Once and For All

Once and For All

A Confession of the Cross

TOM SMAIL

Wipf & Stock
PUBLISHERS
Eugene, Oregon

Wipf and Stock Publishers
199 W 8th Ave, Suite 3
Eugene, OR 97401

Once and for All
A Confession of the Cross
By Smail, Tom
Copyright©1998 by Smail, Tom
ISBN: 1-59244-344-3
Publication date 5/2/2005
Previously published by Darton, Longman and Todd, 1998

For Colin and Valerie
in celebration of a long friendship

Contents

Preface

To write about the cross is, like Jacob at Peniel, to wrestle with something or, rather, with someone, who is totally mysterious and utterly unconquerable – a someone whom you cannot let go because you know that he has it in his power, certainly to wound you at the sore places he exposes, but also to bless you and to change your name and your destiny.

I have been involved in that kind of wrestling with the gospel of the cross for the best part of fifty years of Christian ministry, as I have tried to come to terms with what it means for me, and how I could proclaim its truth to others. This book is one result of that wrestling; it has been an extremely demanding task, and not just on an intellectual level, but I hope that there may be some blessing in it for others in its reading, as there has been much for me in its writing.

I have sub-titled the book 'A Confession of the Cross', because, as I explain in the first chapter, anything one says on such a subject can spring only from a deep personal engagement with it. The book is therefore not a detailed exegesis of biblical passages, although I have tried to give it a sound biblical base. It is neither a history of the doctrine of the atonement, although it relates at many points to that history, nor is it an attempt to commend the atoning work of Christ to those who do not believe or affirm it, although I hope some such may find help in its pages. It is what it says it is, my confession of the cross from the place where I now stand, guided by the scriptures and the many diverse strands of the Christian tradition, Reformed, Catholic and Orthodox, that have become precious to me.

Every chapter has as part of its title the phrase, 'One Cross', because I want to make it clear that what I am discussing is not general truths about life and death, injustice and suffering, sin and forgiveness, but what was revealed and done uniquely and for ever by the Triune God when Jesus Christ hung on a gibbet outside Jerusalem two thousand years ago. It is as we look at what happened once, that we will see that it was indeed for us all.

In the later chapters of the book I have paid special attention to the work of the Holy Spirit in relation to the suffering and death of Jesus which, I have come to see, provides a much needed underpinning of all that we know about the Spirit's work in the Church and its members. There is indeed no Pentecost without Calvary: the Spirit comes from the cross.

My theological debts will become clear from a reading of the book. In its writing I have had the help of our friend, Mary Duncan, who not only examined the proofs with a meticulous eye but also read the whole in draft and made many suggestions, both literary and theological, for its improvement. I am grateful also to Morag Reeve of Darton, Longman & Todd for her support of the project from initial proposal to publication. My wife, Truda, has allowed the leisure of our retirement to be interrupted by my many hours at the computer and has comforted and encouraged all the way through, for love of me, but also for our shared love of the crucified and risen Lord.

TOM SMAIL
London, Epiphany 1998

1

Confessing the One Cross

The cross is like the sun; it gives warmth and light by the unendurable burning at the heart of it; it confers life on others by the destructive forces at work within it that make it a place of relentless dying. It has its own unique location where alone it can be found, but its brightness penetrates to every other place in the many different worlds over which it exercises its gracious influence. Everything living depends on its continued shining even though its face is often obscured. There are clouds that belong to the earthly atmosphere, different kinds of blindness that afflict beholding eyes, a love of darkness and a fear of light that make it hard for the source of all brightness to be acknowledged, far less to be loved.

The comparison, however, can be taken no further. The sun dominates its domain as an impersonal object that does its life-giving work by chemical processes; the cross is at the heart of its kingdom only in virtue of the person who hangs upon it. The life and the light that come from it are shed not by the automatic operation of physical processes, but by the conscious and willed accomplishment of a personal purpose. Jesus is here because he has discerned that life and light can come to the whole of humanity only from this one place, that it is not enough that his brightness should shine from an unapproachable distance like that of the sun. Life must come from the place of death, and light from the densest darkness. Therefore it is only from the eclipse of the cross, where the shadow of the world obscures the brightness of the heavens – it is only from Calvary – that he can savingly shine.

The Elusiveness of the Cross

In these two allusive and perhaps even elusive paragraphs the
main concerns of this book have already begun to emerge. It is
perhaps appropriate that they should be allowed to emerge first
of all in this indirect and figurative way, so that the style of the
writing may point to the character of its subject. The significance
of the work of Christ on the cross is itself so elusive in its mystery
that, from the scriptural beginnings onwards, it can be talked
about only in terms of metaphors and analogies. These are taken,
for example, from the emancipation of slaves, the procedures of
the law courts, the sacrificial practices of Old Testament religion,
to name the three most prominent biblical metaphors. What was
happening on the cross can be described in terms of its resem-
blances to and differences from what was happening in these
other three realms of human activity. But in each case the differences are at least as important as the similarities. Understandings
of atonement can go badly wrong when the likenesses are exag-
gerated and the differences underplayed, as we shall see before
we have done.

Furthermore the use of different metaphors and the refusal of
the Church to commit itself exclusively to one approach to an
understanding of atonement, suggests that no one comparison
can ever be adequate to the whole mystery. Here, most of all
when we focus on Christ crucified, are we forced to confess with
St Paul that what we see are 'puzzling reflections in a mirror'.
Just as it is impossible to look directly at the sun, so it is impossible to grasp completely what Christ is doing on the cross.

Thus to relativise the analogies by which the Church has
sought to understand the work of Christ is by no means to
dismiss them. They cannot say everything, but it is through them
that down the centuries we have been able to say anything and
they have a robustness about them that argues for their suitability
and indeed indispensability for our approach to Calvary. As John
McInytre puts it:

> What we have witnessed in the history of the Church's
> thinking about the death of Christ has been the quite remark-
> able capacity on the part of such models (the biblical
> metaphors of atonement) to root themselves in a vast variety
> of heterogeneous cultures, and to find comprehensible

expression in generations separated from one another sometimes by hundreds of years – and that fact is no less true today than it was 400 or 1500 years ago.[1]

We shall have much to say about such biblical and classical metaphors and models all the way through our study, but at the moment the important point is that the mystery of the crucified Christ surpasses them all. That is why it is always inappropriate to claim to have comprehended that mystery in some all embracing 'theory of atonement' which can then become the sole measure of acceptable soteriological orthodoxy in terms of which everyone and everything that does not speak in conformity with it can be criticised and castigated. That represents a theological arrogance that itself disqualifies its proponents from speaking appropriately about the cross by which all human arrogance is exposed and deposed.

The Blindness of the Beholders

That call to humility, which anybody writing on this subject does well to remember, is reinforced when we recollect that the cross can never be completely comprehended. This is because what happens there is dazzlingly bright beyond our capacity to behold it, and also because there are elements in our circumstances and our seeing that can cloud and qualify our discerning. There is an external cloudiness and an internal lack of focus that can interfere with the view.

Human cultures are cloudy things. They both admit the light and at the same time obscure it. The basic presuppositions, preoccupations, priorities and values of the place and time in which we live deeply affect every one of us far more fundamentally than we usually recognise. That is as true of Christians and theologians as it is of everybody else. We look at the cross as people of our time imbued with the atmosphere of our time and that atmosphere is always cloudy. It does not entirely exclude the light that streams from Calvary but it does filter it often in ways that are obscuring and distorting, although sometimes also in ways that enable us to recognise shades and colours that have not been noticed so clearly in the past.

The obscuring and distorting effect of the two dominant cultures of his day were recognised by Paul right from the start of his apostolic work. He writes to the Corinthians: 'Jews demand miraculous signs and Greeks look for wisdom, but we preach Christ crucified: a stumbling block to Jews and foolishness to Gentiles' (1 Cor. 1:22–3). The Greek preoccupation with intellectual ideas and the Jewish preoccupation with a God of sovereign power made it impossible for them to do anything but despise a salvation that depended upon the work of a condemned criminal on a cross. The cultural cloud was so dense that the light of Calvary could not break through.

It is equally important to recognise that these cultural influences apply in a different way to Christians, for whom the light of the cross has broken through, as is shown by the way in which they seek to interpret what they have seen. For example the atonement theology of the Western Church, both in its medieval Catholic and its reformation Protestant form, has been stated most often and most characteristically in terms of Latin law. As Timothy Gorringe puts it:

> With the translation of the New Testament into Latin, the loss of Byzantium, and the hegemony of Latin as the language of both government and intellectuals, the New Testament was inevitably read through the interpretative lens of the Latin genius, which was law.[2]

Anselm interpreted this in feudal terms in the twelfth century. Dishonour done to an overlord had to be repaid by an appropriate offer of satisfaction if punishment was to be avoided. So Jesus on the cross offers himself to the Father as an infinitely valuable compensation for all the sins of the world. In the sixteenth century the Reformers, still working within the framework of Roman law, saw Christ as bearing the deserved punishment of death for the sins of the world.

The presuppositions of the times rendered these two presentations credible for the people of that time in a way that they are not credible for us at the end of the twentieth century. As we shall see in detail later, our culture wants us to see Christ both as a fellow victim of and as deliverer from the suffering he shares with us, rather than the one who offered satisfaction or bore punishment for sin in our place. The cultural atmosphere is dif-

ferent and so the way we see the cross is different also. To get
more light it may be that as well as seeing what we see in our day
we have to listen very carefully to what our forerunners in the
faith tell us about what they saw in theirs, because what is hidden
from the one may be clearer to the other.

The Spirit and the Scriptures

None of this means that we are the helpless prisoners of our
own culture or that the light of the crucified Christ cannot break
through the factors that obscure it from us. We may have much
need to be humble about the finality or the completeness of our
seeing, but we have no need to despair about the possibility
of seeing anything at all. As the sun is mightier than the clouds,
so the cross is stronger than the culture. It is precisely in the
context in which Paul has been speaking of the obscuring effect of
human culture on the message of the cross that he also speaks
of the power of the Holy Spirit to reveal that message to God's
people:

> The Spirit searches all things, even the deep things of God.
> For who among men knows the thoughts of a man except the
> man's spirit within him? In the same way no one knows
> the thoughts of God except the Spirit of God. We have not
> received the spirit of the world but the Spirit who is from
> God, that we may understand what God has freely given us.
> This is what we speak, not in words taught us by human
> wisdom but in words taught by the Spirit, expressing spiri-
> tual truths in spiritual words. (1 Cor. 2:10–13)

We may never master the mystery that is enacted on Calvary
because it is too deep for us, but the promise is that God's Spirit
does not leave us cut off from it by the spirit of the world and its
culture but is constantly at work in the Church to lead us out of
the one atmosphere into the other, from the world that is dominated by the power of culture to the world that is dominated by
the power of the cross. The Spirit of God opens the deep things of
God to the people of God. That is one reason why confession
of the cross requires far more than historical knowledge or a

theological bent. The indispensable qualification is a humble openness to and prayer for the illumination of the Spirit, 'Come Holy Spirit, and show us the Lord.' In the high pressure zone where the Spirit operates, there may not be clear skies but there is a promise of constant breaks in the clouds. A Christian theology of the cross must be a charismatic theology – one that depends on the Spirit's coming and the Spirit's working most of all.

As he answers that prayer the Spirit will send us back to the scriptures and especially the apostolic scriptures of the New Testament where the message of the cross has its first and classic formulation. The Paul who wrote to Corinth knew Jesus Christ and him crucified with such a concentrated loyalty that he was able to confront, challenge and correct the controlling cultures of the world in which he was working. However, Paul always did this in a way that offered them in Christ the fulfilment of what they had been looking for apart from Christ. If the Greeks wanted wisdom, then the place where the supreme wisdom was to be found was at Calvary; if the Jews wanted demonstrations of power, then the mightiest power in all the world was the love of the crucified and risen Lord.

The apostolic word of the cross is, in the power of the Spirit, able both to judge and to fulfil the cultures that it encounters and our faith and hope is that it will do so still. It is therefore our business as people of our time, influenced as we certainly are by the culture of our time, to trust the Holy Spirit and to turn to the apostolic witness to Christ crucified. In that way the message of the cross may again confront, challenge and correct the cultural preoccupations and presuppositions that we bring to it.

We are on the one hand to use the light that our culture has to lead us into the fuller light that shines from Calvary. We shall in fact soon see that our day has its own distinctive contribution to make to a theology of the cross. On the other hand we need to be rescued from at least some of the darkness with which our culture, like all others, diminishes and distorts the shining that stems from the cross, and we shall find contemporary evidence of that also. The clouds both transmit and obscure the light of the sun and it is the business of the Holy Spirit to use the light that we have and to restore the light that we have lost or never had.

Inner Darkness Exposed

Before we pursue that twin task in greater detail, we have to recognise that our relationship to the crucified Jesus is obscured not only by cultural cloudiness but even more by inner darkness and the blindness that results from it. The nearer you get to the sun, the more you are exposed to its all-revealing light and its burning heat. The nearer you get to the cross, the more your disguises are penetrated, the more transparent it becomes what kind of person you really are. As Jesus himself put it: 'This is the verdict: Light has come into the world, but men loved darkness instead of light because their deeds were evil. Everyone who does evil hates the light, and will not come into the light for fear that his deeds will be exposed' (John 3:19–20). That hatred of the light and that fear of exposure by it are, thank God, not the last word about any of us, but it is a real factor for all of us. As we shall go on seeing throughout the book, God's love for us in Christ highlights almost intolerably all sorts of things in us that defy and deny that love. What he had to do for us to save us from our plight underlines the direness of our need and our inability to cope with it.

This needs much fuller and more theological explication, but it has a personal dimension to it that is a real factor in our thinking about the cross. There is in me that which does not want to think about the cross at all, that which wants to pass quickly from it to the triumphs of Easter or the excitements of Pentecost. If I do I shall be yielding to what Martin Luther rightly saw as the inveterate tendency of the human heart to avoid a *theologia crucis*, a theology that has the cross at the centre, and hasten immediately to a *theologia gloriae* that bypasses the cross. There is that in me and, I suspect, in all of us that wants to deny its centrality and diminish its significance, because it is at the cross that I am judged and found wanting, my self-esteem is shaken, my pride humiliated and my ultimate moral standing radically questioned. The crucified Jesus is the judge of all the earth. He was the judge of all who surrounded him on Calvary and he is the judge of all those who look in the direction of Calvary and know that they were there when they crucified the Lord. We must be careful that that powerful desire to protect ourselves from that judgement does not express itself in an

evasion of the cross in our theology, in our worship, in our
Christian living.

The Attraction of the Crucified Christ

But if, like Peter and the first disciples, our original reaction is to
run from the cross, the crucified Jesus constantly draws us back
to himself. The two reactions are encapsulated in what he says
about his coming death: 'Now is the time for judgement on this
world; now the prince of this world will be driven out. But I,
when I am lifted up from the earth, will draw all men to myself'
(John 12:31–2). It is at the heart of the Christian experience down
the centuries and across the continents that the fear of the suffering that is explicit and of the judgement that is implicit at
Calvary is more than counteracted by the drawing power of the
holy love that is mysteriously acting on our behalf at Calvary.
Again and again the love that streams from the crucified Jesus
attracts us to him and persuades us again and again not to run
away. He shows us that only by what he has done there can our
most fundamental need be first measured and then met. The
sharpness of the judgement that repels us is only the sharpness of
the surgeon's knife whose one aim is our healing and renewal
into a quality of life that is different from anything we have yet
known:

> The wounded surgeon plies the steel
> That questions the distempered part;
> Beneath the bleeding hands we feel
> The sharp compassion of the healer's art[3]

Confessing the Cross

We can speak validly of the saving work of Christ on the cross
only when we have in some measure submitted to the judgement
that he passes upon us and surrendered to the love that alone is
able to heal us. A theology of the cross can never be a detached
intellectual exercise by someone who is not personally involved

in what he is speaking about. It is not enough to collate the
teaching of scripture and work it into a systematic scheme or to
subject the atonement teaching of the Church to a cool critical
assessment. The sacrifice of Christ of which we speak involves for
him a total act of self-giving and we shall be able to make an
appropriate response to that sacrifice only in our own responsive
and ever deepening act of self-giving. That is an entirely scriptural statement; the chief qualification of the first great theologian
of the cross was that he knew for himself 'the Son of God who
loved me and gave himself for me' (Gal. 2:20) and all the implications that that had for him. *Crux probat omnia*, the cross tests
everything, said Luther, and among those who are tested most by
it are its would be interpreters.

I have noticed over the years as I have struggled again and
again with my own understanding of what Christ was about on
Calvary, and have sometimes attained relative clarity and sometimes lost it, that my understanding or lack of it was subtly but
powerfully related to my own spiritual state. My mind began to
lose its grasp of Christ's truth when my life was out of harmony
with his will and his purpose, but the nearer I was to him, the
more insight I had into what he had done for me and for
the world. The perceptiveness of the theology both affected and
was itself affected by the reality of the relationship. The nearer
I was drawn to him personally, the more my thinking, feeling and
acting were being shaped by the same love that died for me on
Calvary, and the more I was able to grasp in my thinking and
speaking the length and breadth and depth and height of what
his love was involved in doing there, not just for me but for the
world.

The writing of this book, therefore, is not just a theological
exercise but part of one person's whole response to the crucified
and risen Lord. It falls under the rubric of Romans 12:

> Therefore, I urge you, brothers, in view of God's mercy, to
> offer your bodies as living sacrifices, holy and pleasing
> to God – this is your spiritual act of worship. Do not conform
> any longer to the pattern of this world, but be transformed
> by the renewing of your mind. Then you will be able to test
> and approve what God's will is – his good, pleasing and
> perfect will. (Rom. 12:1–2)

The ability to escape from conformity with the cloudy culture that controls us, to have our minds transformed and renewed so that we are capable of catching at least valid glimpses of God's great purpose achieved in the death of Jesus, all that depends on our being so moved by the mercy of God that gave itself for us on Calvary that we are enabled at least in some measure to give ourselves to him.

In the Christian community personal relationship is always prior to theological statement; we know about God only when we know God, just as in human relationships what I say about a person is most securely based when I know that person. If that is true across the whole field of Christian belief, it is pre-eminently true in relation to the atoning work of Christ. What is at issue there is precisely our personal relationship with God, where we are most radically disturbed by his judgement and transformed by his redeeming act.

Here the split between theology and spirituality, between what we think and how we pray, that bedevils so much contemporary Christian thinking and acting is shown to be totally impossible, because at every turn the one affects the other. For example, how seriously I speak of sin and what it takes to overcome sin is inseparable from my own dealings with God on these very subjects. If the theology of the cross is the theology of a restored relationship then those who write about it or read and assess what is written about it show to what degree they are or are not involved in that relationship.

In other words, the theology of the cross is always a confessional theology and that is what I take myself to be attempting in this book. What I offer is one man's confession of Christ crucified, a confession that has been struggled with for forty years as I have tried to understand it for myself and proclaim it to others. Indeed it is being struggled with again in the very act of writing about it. Like Jacob at Peniel one is continually closing with the mysterious stranger, knowing that he has the key to the future and crying to him both 'I will not let you go till you bless me' and 'Tell me your name'. In that struggle we are like Jacob both wounded and made whole.

Three Confessions

(a) The Confession of Faith

The theology of the cross is confessional in three distinct senses. Firstly it makes a claim of faith that is founded on an act of trust in Jesus Christ as the object of that faith. Apart from that act of trust the confession has no basis and for those who cannot share that act of trust it has little meaning. It is a decision to read the events of the world's life and of one's own life in the light of the crucified and risen Jesus. One can then try to show how that makes more sense of them than any other possible reading and hope that that claim will be persuasive and able to give credible answers to the objections that are made to it. That persuasion will however fall far short of proof; there will be alternative readings that are still possible, issues that are still unsettled, questions that have no final answers. As Bishop Lesslie Newbigin never tires of reminding us, as Christians we are witnesses to what we have seen, not judges and juries pronouncing verdicts. We must go on claiming that our confession is not only credible but that the one that we confess is the ultimate truth for the whole world, because that is what we have seen. We must do so humbly remembering that his truth and credibility will be established, as Paul knew well, not by persuasive words or arguments, but by the Spirit of the risen and crucified Lord, whom we confess and on whom we totally depend for the truth of our confession.

(b) The Confession of Sin

But the confession of faith at the cross has to be simultaneously the confession of sin at the cross. In the presence of the crucified Jesus I stand not primarily as the trained academic theologian or as God's friend and defender, but as the one who sees here what I myself am really like and what needed to be done in order that I may stand in the presence of God at all. The only one who can know anything of the saving mystery of the cross is the one who has been judged and humbled at the cross. 'O break, O break, hard heart of mine! Thy weak self-love and guilty pride his Pilate and his Judas were, Jesus, our Lord, is crucified.'

(c) The Confession of Praise

However we need also to see that the confession of faith and of
sin lead on immediately to a release of praise at the cross in which
they are not abolished but subsumed. If the confession of faith is
a witness to the world and the confession of sin concerns us,
the praise is directed to God. Here the confident humility of the
witness and the shamed humility of the sinner are caught up into
the wonder of what God in Christ has done for the world and
for the sinners; here the humility is the gateway to the glorying.
The writer to the Colossians delineates the primary response of
Christians to the gospel of the cross as: 'joyfully giving thanks to
the Father, who has qualified you to share in the inheritance
of the saints in the kingdom of light. For he has rescued us from
the dominion of darkness and brought us into the kingdom of the
Son he loves, in whom we have redemption, the forgiveness of
sins' (Col. 1:12–14).

Everything that the New Testament says about atonement is
suffused with praise; it is theological doxology, it is, in terms of
Romans 12:1–3, a renewing of the mind to engage in a spiritual
worship that is pleasing to God. It is, like the Eucharist at the
heart of it, the response of overflowing gratitude to unbounded
and unconditional grace. A theology that does not sing is bad
theology. A theology of the cross, however scriptural, learned
and orthodox, that does not pulsate with the thrill of sins forgiven and life renewed by the self-giving love of God in Christ is
unworthy of its object and untrue to its biblical sources. 'Thanks
be to God for his indescribable gift!' (2 Cor. 9:15).

What follows is intended to be confessional in all these three
senses, by someone who, despite all the clouds and blindness,
has seen the life-giving light of God shining from that cross, who
has been humbled by it and, as part of his praiseful response to it,
wants to give his mind with all the rigour and concentration that
he can summon, to understand it and to expound it as clearly as
he can.

Confession and Tradition

Such a confession must by its very nature be personal. The creeds of the Church hang in the air until people own them, until either a personal 'I believe' or a corporate 'We believe' anchors them. A faith has to be somebody's faith; a confession has to have its confessors. But to be personal is not to be individualistic. My believing must be something I do *for* myself if it is to have any reality, but it can never be something that I do *by* myself in isolation from my relationships with others and with the whole people of God. The contents of the Creeds are not the works of individuals, they are given to us from outside ourselves to be owned and made our own when we add, as it were, our name to them. What *I* believe is what the Church has believed long before me. The gospel is not conveyed by internal mystical enlightenment, but by God's entering into relationships with people in earthly time and space. It is therefore to be conveyed to people through time and space, through historical tradition, the handing on of the good news from one community to another on the large scale and from one person to another on the small.

This book springs from my personal appropriation of that tradition and my minuscule part in the interpretation of that tradition, as I seek to transmit it to others. Without that reception of what the tradition has given me, I would have nothing to confess. People are who they are by virtue of their relationships with one another: Christians are who they are and believe what they believe in virtue of a whole set of relationships with the culture that surrounds them and with the tradition of the Christian community to which they belong.

What is offered here therefore is the personal confession of a man who is living and writing at the turn of the millennium, in the context of the culture of this place and time, and seeking from that place and time to receive and restate the good news of Christ crucified that comes to me in the tradition of the Church to which I belong. That means that this confession will have universal features common to the whole Christian tradition, specific features belonging to the form in which that tradition has reached me, and personal features that emerge from the way in which the universal truth has impacted on someone of my shape, background and personal predilections.

A Scriptural Confession

From that position I make my confession of Christ crucified. My primary contact with Christ is through the scriptures of the New Testament in which the person and the culminating event of his life and their significance are presented to me in close connection with the scriptures of the Old Testament which, it is claimed, the person and the event completes and fulfils. To ensure therefore that I am confessing the same Christ and the same cross that the apostles confessed and not some private Jesus of my own shaping, I have at every point to submit my confession to the witness of the scriptures, to make as sure as I can that what I am saying in my time and way is at every point consonant with what they have said before in theirs. My personal idiosyncrasies and my cultural presuppositions have alike to be submitted to the judgement of the written word of God, because it is only through the written word that I have contact with the living Word who died on Calvary.

Submitting to the scriptures, of course, goes far beyond backing my statements with biblical texts. It means that I must take account of the diversity of approaches with which the biblical writers interpret the event of the cross and try to do justice to them all. It means also that I have to look at the cross in the particular context in which the gospel writers view it. The death of Jesus is the culmination of the life of Jesus and is almost immediately followed by the resurrection of Jesus; it cannot be understood except in terms of what went before it and led up to it and what came afterwards and cast floods of light on it.

Furthermore through his life, his death and his rising, Jesus raises the question of his person: who was it that so lived, so died, so rose again? What we say about his person will both affect and be affected by what we say about his cross. If we say he is the Son of God, we shall be asked what kind of God this was who handed over his Son to suffering and death. If on the other hand we deny his divinity we shall not be able to claim that on the cross he did for us what only God could do and that his death and his resurrection were the eschatological moment of the rescuing of the old creation and the inauguration of the new.

A Trinitarian Confession

Such questions arise from the biblical witness and are given their classical answers in the credal tradition of the Church, with its central Christian claim that the New Testament is rightly interpreted only when Jesus is understood as the incarnate Son, the eternal Word made flesh for our salvation. That tradition claims that his story is to be read as the revelation of the Triune God, the Father who sent, the Son who came, the Spirit who draws us into relationship with them and participation in the one life that they share. My confession is not only a biblical but also an ecclesial confession, made by a member of the Church who adheres to the creeds of the Church. It therefore has to take into account the credal claims that the cross is the act of the Incarnate Son performed in obedience to his Father and resulting in the release of the Holy Spirit. As I make my confession I have to go on asking myself whether and how the Incarnational Trinitarian creed of the Church helps or hinders me in my knowledge of and contact with Christ crucified and risen. In such resubmissions of the theology of the creeds to the authority of scripture the faith of the Church is constantly to be corrected and refreshed from its biblical source.

In recent theology the German theologian, Jürgen Moltmann, has most helpfully reasserted the intimate connection between the cross and the Triune God in his seminal book, *The Crucified God*. Moltmann can startle those for whom the doctrine of the Trinity was a piece of irrelevant theological mumbo jumbo or a presumptuous intrusion into the inner life of God, by such statements as the following:

> If the cross of Jesus is understood as a divine event, i.e. as an event between Jesus and his God and Father, it is necessary to speak in Trinitarian terms of the Son and the Father and the Spirit. In that case the doctrine of the Trinity is no longer an exorbitant and impractical speculation about God, but is *nothing other than a shorter version of the passion narrative of Christ*.[4] (Italics mine)

One might argue with the 'nothing other' in that last sentence, but the claim of intimate connection between cross and Trinity must certainly stand. We shall begin to understand the cross only

if we affirm on the one hand that Jesus is 'of one being with the
Father' and that it is none other than God himself who suffered
with us and dies for us. And yet at the same time we must allow
such a distinction of persons between Son and Father as will
allow us to take seriously the Lord's cry of desolation: 'My God,
my God, why have you abandoned me?' We shall have much
more to say about that as we proceed but note that the doctrine of
the Trinity *prima facie* at least allows for both the divine unity
and the distinction that the theology of the cross requires.[5]

One of the criticisms of Moltmann at this point is that while he
had much to say about how the cross defined the relationships
between Father and Son, he had much less to say about the Holy
Spirit in this connection. He might have replied that the New
Testament documents had even less, and it is certainly true that
where scripture is nearly – but not quite – silent, we need to be
reticent in what we say. Nevertheless as convinced Trinitarians
we cannot evade the question about the relation of the Spirit to
the suffering and dying of the Son and we shall be taking it up in
a later chapter.

These are some of the questions that arise when we allow
scripture and tradition to interact as we seek to come to terms
with the cross. The way we answer them will have very practical
implications for our worship and for our understanding of the
life of discipleship.

The Centrality of Calvary

In the life of the Church creeds and confessions usually arise
when Christians needs to reassert some central aspect of the faith
which has been obscured or distorted either by the prevailing
church tradition or because it is uncongenial to the culture of the
day. My own confession of the cross has a similar concern,
because as this book's title, with all its nuances indicates, my
chief concern is to reassert the uniqueness and centrality for the
whole of humanity at all times and in all places of what happened only once in human history: when Jesus of Nazareth was
crucified outside Jerusalem during the Procuratorship of Pontius
Pilate. On what he did then in our absence, our present and our
future salvation totally depends.

That is not a message that is much emphasised or acknowledged in large sections of the Church today, although it is still formally affirmed in our creeds and liturgies. It is a message that the culture of the day finds very hard to cope with. The claim that someone else has done for us what we cannot do for ourselves is seen as an attack on our autonomy and an attempt to deprive us of our freedom. The further claim that the decisive moment for the world and for our own present and future lies in the distant past is unacceptable to a generation that prizes present experience above past tradition, and that discounts what happened yesterday in favour of what can happen today. And, most outrageous of all, is the challenge to our cherished cultural diversity and religious pluralism in the claim that there is one universal source from which salvation comes, one story about one man to which everyone else is called to relate.

That distancing from the one gospel of the one cross goes on inside the Church as well. Problematic theologies of atonement that expounded in unacceptable ways how the dying of Christ affected the whole of humanity have often, by reaction, led to views of the cross in which its uniquely saving efficacy is minimised. Experience of the Spirit has for many become more central than faith in the Crucified, so that the Christian centre has been moved from Calvary to Pentecost.

This emphasis on salvation as our present experience rather than on Christ's atoning work is echoed in the type of atonement theology represented by Paul Fiddes, in *Past Event and Present Salvation*. Here, the traditional Christian claim that God has saved there and then through the work of Christ is consistently played down in favour of the experiential alternative that God does save here and now through Christ. He writes:

> Salvation happens here and now. It is always in the present that God acts to heal and reconcile, entering into the disruption of human lives at great cost to himself, in order to share our predicament and rescue us from it.[6]

The emphasis in such a statement contrasts vividly with the Pauline emphasis on the 'God who has reconciled us to himself through Christ' (2 Cor. 5:18), where the act of reconciliation has been completed for us in the past long before it is announced to us in the present, and our experienced participation in it, vital as it is, is a result of relating ourselves to what was done for us long ago. In terms of Fiddes' title the present salvation has its whole source and efficacy in the past event. I must trust in what Christ has done *for* me before I can be open to what he will begin to do *in* me. Thus briefly stated, that might look like a theological quibble but the burden of this book is to expound it and to show again in our day that, whether our culture likes it or not, it is on the finished work of Christ on Calvary that the whole gospel depends. Through many clouds, despite much blindness, the Son shines and he shines most brightly from the blackness of his cross.

2

One Cross – Four Gospels

To make contact with Christ crucified we have to start with scripture, and first of all with the four gospels. It will take all the resources of both Old and New Testaments to interpret the meaning of the cross, but it is only the gospels that offer us detailed narratives of what actually happened at Calvary, what led up to it and what followed from it. Without that narrative there would be nothing to interpret and every later interpretation, whether in the letters of Paul or the atonement theology of the Church, has to authenticate itself by giving a credible account of what that narrative was really about. A theory of atonement that is out of relation to the historical record of what Jesus did and saw himself to be doing in his death is disqualified by that fact. Furthermore, if we are claiming that this event in its historical specificity is of universal significance, so that the salvation of the world depends upon it, it is of special importance that we should try to ascertain as best we can what kind of event this really was. For that our only source is the gospels.

One of the things that recent biblical scholarship has taught us is that the distinction between narrative and interpretation is only relative. To tell a story in a certain way is to offer an interpretation of it. The gospel narratives are full of clues to the meaning of what was happening when Jesus died, in terms, for example, of Old Testament allusions and the recounting of details like the rending of the temple veil which have immense symbolic importance.

One Story: Four Gospels

When we compare the story as the four evangelists recount it, we are left in no doubt that it is the same story about the same man dying on the same cross that they are telling. As has often been noted, all four gospels are organised in such a way that the last week and the last day of Jesus' life is allocated a vastly disproportionate amount of space. This is their way of telling us that what happened there at that time is the centre and culmination of everything that went before, and therefore requires a much more extended account.

We are however equally aware that each tells the story of what happened on these last crucial days in a quite distinctive way. It is not being suggested that any of them is trying to impose upon the event a meaning that is alien to it, but rather that each is concerned to highlight one aspect of what is going on, perhaps because it was that aspect that the evangelist considered most important to himself or to the first readers to whom his gospel was addressed. He presents his account of the crucifixion and the days that immediately preceded it in a way that ensures that his readers, whether in his own time or in ours, will, at least for the moment, give their full attention to that which he sees to be the most significant aspect of it.

In other words the dark stage of Calvary is swept by four penetrating gospel searchlights, each of which picks out a series of sometimes coinciding and sometimes diverging details in a way that builds up the kind of picture of the crucified Christ that each evangelist wants us to see. We defeat their intention if, in the interests of constructing a unified story, we too quickly try to superimpose these pictures on each other. When we fail to take proper account of the distinctiveness of what the four gospels want to tell us, we are in danger of ending up with a vague and blurred picture in which everything is out of focus and has lost its sharpness.

That can happen through a careless reading of the gospels that misses the particularities of what each wants to say to us, and we can be grateful to contemporary redaction criticism for correcting us at just that point. Perhaps more typically for most of us, it can happen through the kind of liturgical harmonisation that, for example, leads us to speak of Jesus' seven words from the cross without noticing that in Matthew and Mark he speaks just once, or that Luke and John have three sayings that no other gospel records. Far from being an irrelevant detail, the distribution of sayings is of considerable importance because in each gospel the sayings from the cross that it records points us to the aspect of the cross that that gospel wants to underline.

I propose therefore that we should first of all give our full attention to the account of Jesus' death as given by each evangelist in turn, so that without distraction we can hear from him what he wants to tell us about the cross of Jesus. We must then locate that account in the historical context in which it belongs. Only then can we try to put together what we have learnt from the four portraits and come to a rounded three-dimensional appreciation of the man and the event that does justice to them all and that tries to discern from his words and actions what he thought he was doing when he went up to Jerusalem to die.

To that task we now turn. This is not a work of biblical exegesis and there is no room, even if I had the competence, for a verse by verse exposition of the passion narratives of the four gospels, still less for tackling all the critical problems that have been raised about them. These tasks have been undertaken in great detail by the commentators and most recently by Raymond E. Brown.[1] We must be content with the much more modest aim of identifying the main features in the portrait of Jesus in the days and hour of his passion, that each evangelist wants to present to us, to make sure that our confession of Christ crucified takes due account of them all.

We spoke earlier of four distinctive accounts of the passion in the four gospels, but, for our purposes, Matthew and Mark are so similar to each other and so different from Luke and John that, in a summary like this, they can quite properly be looked at together. We therefore have three presentations to which we might give the following titles: for Mark and Matthew, Jesus in his isolation and abandonment; for Luke, Jesus in his saving compassion; and for John, Jesus the final and universal Judge and Saviour.

The Cross in Mark and Matthew

In Mark and Matthew the darkness that surrounds the cross is almost unbroken. The one cry that escapes from the crucified Jesus says it all: 'My God, my God, why have you forsaken me?' Such a word would be quite alien to the narrative of both Luke and John and neither betrays any awareness of it. For Mark it is however central and of all the words of Jesus must have the highest claim to authenticity. There could be no conceivable reason to invent it when, at first sight, it seemed to undermine every claim that the gospels that recorded it wanted to make for him. How could he be the Messiah, the Son of the living God, whom Peter had confessed at Caesarea Philippi, if he died lamenting that the very God he had come to represent had abandoned him? The debate that has surrounded that word down the centuries betrays something of the same embarrassment over it. We shall have much to say about what it means and what it does not mean later, but at the moment it may stand as a summary of what Mark and Matthew want to say about Jesus on the cross.

Everyone has turned from the Markan Jesus – he is totally forsaken by earth and by heaven. He is forsaken by his closest friends, betrayed by Judas, denied by Peter and abandoned by all his disciples at the moment of his arrest: 'Then everyone deserted him and fled' (Mark 14:50). The representative leaders of his own people forsake him. His messianic claim is denied as blasphemy and he is handed over to the Gentile power of Rome to be executed as one who is cast out from the chosen people. He is forsaken by Roman justice, whose representative, Pilate, clearly sees his innocence but retreats from his not-guilty verdict and his attempts to rescue Jesus under pressure from the Jewish leaders and the organised clamour of the crowd. The crowds at the foot of the cross mock him and his fellow victims turn upon him. In the same way the chief priests and the teachers of the law assail him with their taunts: ' "He saved others," they said, "but he can't save himself! Let this Christ, this King of Israel, come down now from the cross, that we may see and believe." Those crucified with him also heaped insults on him' (Mark 15:31–2).

It is therefore the culmination of this abandonment that he should cry out that he has been abandoned not only by men but by his Father, that the relationship that has until now been at the heart of everything for him, from which he has derived the meaning, the guidance and the sustenance for all that he has done, has been broken. He is cut off from *Abba* in whom he has trusted and whose will it has been his first concern to fulfil (Mark 14:36) most of all just here on the cross, and he is utterly desolate and totally alone.

It is a devastatingly dark picture that is relieved only after he has died by the two signs that suggest that in this dense darkness a great work of God is being performed: the tearing apart of the temple curtain that closed off access to the divine presence, and the acknowledgement and confession that came from the last place from which it might have been expected: the Roman officer in charge of the execution. 'The curtain of the temple was torn in two from top to bottom. And when the centurion, who stood there in front of Jesus, heard his cry and saw how he died, he said, "Surely this man was the Son of God!"' (Mark 15:38–9).

Even such a brief outline of the Markan passion narrative is enough to show us how the one word from the cross that Mark records encapsulates the whole thrust of the story he tells. At the beginning of his gospel the evangelist hails him and at the end the centurion confesses him as Son of God. For Mark, however, to be Son of God involves this complete abandonment, when human persons and institutions seem to conspire with his heavenly Father to break off every positive relationship with him and bring about a death of utter forsakenness.

It is of this forsakenness rather than the physical pain that he complains from the cross. It is precisely in his forsakenness, however, that he is the companion of all the abandoned victims of injustice and oppression of which the world has been full right to our own day. Here he joins the company of those who have looked for help from what appeared to be a stony, silent and unresponding heaven and have had their hearts broken because rescue has been denied and support removed, because every relationship that might have supplied them has been broken. The God-forsaken Jesus on the cross joins the company of the God-forsaken. This very fact, as Mark hints by the torn temple curtain, means that for them access to God is again made possible and that, as the centurion amazingly discerned, this very identification is the clinching proof that Jesus is the Son of God.

The Cross in Luke

To turn from Mark and Matthew to Luke is to stay with the cross but to escape from much of the darkness. As Raymond E. Brown puts it:

> ... there is much less of the negative in Luke's presentation of the passion. If for Mark/Matthew victimisation and failure dominate a passion where sudden reversal by God comes only after Jesus' death, for Luke the healing and forgiving power of God is already active in the passion before Jesus' death.[2]

Luke records three words of Jesus from the cross and, in contrast to Mark, they are all words about relationships restored and affirmed rather than relationships broken. In the first and the last Jesus affirms his relationships with his Father. To quote Brown again:

> Readers are given the sense that Jesus is in communion with his Father throughout, so that appropriately the last words of the crucified are not an anguished cry to his God by one who feels forsaken, but a tranquil 'Father, into your hands I place my spirit.'[3]

If that last word expresses a continuing and unbroken communion with and trust in his Father even in death, the first two show that the ministry of Jesus on the cross is one of restoring relationships in his saving compassion, first for his crucifiers and then for the man who was crucified with him and, at the fifty-ninth minute of the eleventh hour, turned to him.

According to Luke, Jesus' first word from the cross was, 'Father, forgive them, for they do not know what they are doing' (Luke 23:34). No doubt the immediate reference is to the soldiers who were his crucifiers, but Jesus looks beyond them to all who have conspired in his death, who by their action represent the whole of our fallen and therefore God-crucifying humanity. He thus makes the cross an act of intercession expressed in this prayer for them all.

That it is an utterly undeserved and unconditionally gracious act is emphasised by his startling exchange with the criminal on the other cross, 'Then [the criminal] said, "Jesus, remember me when you come into your kingdom." Jesus answered him, "I tell you the truth, today you will be with me in paradise"' (Luke 23:42–3). The authority of Jesus to forgive and restore relationships is not related to our past record or our future amendment, to the informedness of our faith or its ability to work itself out in a changed life. There is nobody so far gone that it is too late to turn to Jesus and to turn to the crucified is to enter immediately into a restored relationship which it is entirely in his gift to bestow. It was good Lukan theology that Charlotte Elliott expressed when she said, 'Just as I am, thou wilt receive, wilt welcome, pardon, cleanse, relieve, because thy promise I believe, O Lamb of God I come.' Difficult exegetical and theological questions about the meaning of 'today' and 'paradise' need to be faced and answered, but should not distract us from the amazing grace that the crucified Jesus shows. Having prayed for forgiveness with his first word, he is able to bestow it with his second.

In Luke the centurion at the cross also has the last word, although it has a different nuance, 'The centurion, seeing what had happened, praised God and said, "Surely this was a righteous man"' (Luke 23:47). If 'righteous' in this context has its full biblical meaning, denoting not just personal innocence but the ability to make things right, then the Lukan centurion has more evident grounds for his verdict than his Markan counterpart, because in the gospel according to Luke that is exactly what Jesus is doing from the cross.

The Cross in John

The forsaken Jesus is also the compassionate Jesus of Luke. Before we ask how these can be held together we must first look at John. Here again the same story is told but from a quite different perspective. As Brown puts it: 'Whereas the Jesus of Mark/Matthew is mocked on the cross, and the Jesus of Luke is forgiving, the Jesus of John is triumphant.'[4] His death indeed heralds the arrival of the final eschatological triumph of God and bears all its marks. The keywords within which the Johannine passion are set are the great word with which he enters Jerusalem on Palm Sunday, '"Now is the time for judgement on this world;

now the prince of this world will be driven out. But I, when I am lifted up from the earth, will draw all men to myself." He said this to show the kind of death he was going to die' (John 12:31–3). The final cry of triumph with which he gives up his spirit on the cross is an eschatological word that speaks of the end-time triumph of the saving purposes of God. 'When he had received the drink, Jesus said, "It is finished." With that, he bowed his head and gave up his spirit' (John 19:30). *Tetelstai* is less a cry of termination than of achievement. It is all accomplished, everything that needed to be done has been done and now it can all begin to work on a universal scale.

In Jewish eschatology the end-time was marked by the last judgement and the Johannine Jesus sees that that last judgement has been executed by his death. But it is a judgement that is not a condemnation but a redeeming act that has in it the power to put right everything that is wrong with the world and the people in it in a universal way, 'I will draw all men to myself.' The camera, as it were, zooms back from the particular context of Calvary and sets the cross against the vast cosmic context of universal destiny.

Furthermore the end-time was to be marked by the outpouring of the Spirit and it is significant that in one of John's frequent *double entendres* he tells us how Jesus bows his head and hands over his Spirit. He hands it over to his Father now that his work is accomplished, but also to the embryonic disciple company: his mother, the disciples whom he loved, his aunt Mary Cleopas, and Mary Magdalene, the last remnant of the old Israel and the first promise of the new. From the cross he gives the disciple company the Spirit who makes all things new, the Spirit that is symbolised as always in this gospel[5] by the water that pours from his side with the blood of his self-giving when his body is pierced by the soldier's spear. The same Spirit in this same paschal context is to be breathed upon the disciples after the risen Jesus has showed them the hands and the side wounded on the cross (John 20:22).

In the death of Jesus and in the light of his resurrection the long awaited last things have started to happen and that makes his cross into a throne. His being lifted up to die on Calvary is already a foreshadowing of his being lifted up to live at Easter and his being lifted up to reign in his Ascension. In John he is triumphing as he is dying, he remains in control of the situation even when to outward appearances he seems a helpless victim. The prisoner they are judging himself judges both the Jews and

Pilate. The same Pilate who is cynical about truth is ironically the one who tells the truth about the cross when he has erected over it in all the languages of that ancient world, 'Jesus of Nazareth, the king of the Jews'.

The first two words from the cross in the Johannine record are worth comparing with those in Mark and Luke. This Jesus, as we have already said, is not alone in his dying, a small but faithful company is already gathered at the foot of the cross. Jesus inaugurates new relationships, not this time as in Luke with the criminal who is far outside the disciple company, but within it. The Johannine commandment to Christians is not so much that they should love their enemies as that they should love one another. So here with his dying breath he forges new relationships between his mother and the disciple who has been closest to him and who in this gospel represents the Church that is to come: 'When Jesus saw his mother there, and the disciple whom he loved standing near by, he said to his mother, "Dear woman, here is your son," and to the disciple, "Here is your mother." From that time on, this disciple took her into his home' (John 19:26–7). The Church maternal (Mary) is to be received into the home of the Church apostolic (John), the pastoral and theological belong together. Mary, because she is the mother of Jesus, is to be honoured as the mother of the brothers and sisters of Jesus. To expound all that in detail would be to stray too far from our central purpose, but, according to John, that kind of relationship is being forged at the cross.

The second word from the cross in this gospel is 'I am thirsty' and here John makes contact with Mark and remembers that the triumph that he wants to emphasise is being won in a context of dire need and deprivation. The king of Israel on his cross–throne is also a parched and dehydrated man suffering a thirst that we well-watered Westerners have never experienced. His cry of thirst is the expression of his pain. In its Johannine context the word is introduced as a fulfilment of scripture, and commentators have suggested various verses from the psalms of which it might be an echo. The first verses of Psalm 42 suggest that the thirst referred to here is not only a physical thirst for a drink but also a spiritual thirst for fellowship with God.

As the deer pants for streams of water, so my soul pants for you, O God.

My soul thirsts for God, for the living God.
When can I go and meet with God?
My tears have been my food day and night,
  while men say to me all day long, 'Where is your God?'
                                          (Psalm 42:1–3)

If that is anywhere near John's understanding of this cry of Jesus,
it brings it into contact with the Markan cry of forsakenness. The
king on the cross is thirsting with all his being for a restoration of
his undimmed fellowship with his Father.

The Gospels Together – The Full Story

We have identified in the gospels three portraits of the dying
Jesus, each of which is quite distinctive and in some tension with
the other two, as becomes clear when we compare Mark with
John. Our first and perhaps typically modern reaction to this
diversity of approaches is to try to get behind the gospel presentations to 'what really happened'; to look from the portraits
slowly drawn in recollection of what happened on the day to the
snapshot taken immediately on the day. Or, if that is not available, we might seek to construct arguments that would make one
of the portraits more authentic to the original than the other two
and thus to decide what Jesus actually said from what has been
put on his lips by the earliest Christian tradition in its post-Easter
attempts to formulate a gospel that had the cross at its centre.

Both of these are highly dubious enterprises. We know nothing
of the event of Calvary except what the gospels tell us and it is
more important to listen to their witness to that event than to
speculate about which of them may have more accurately pro-
duced the historical details of it. One does not need to be a
blinkered fundamentalist to have faith that God has seen to it that
all the gospels together tell us what we need to know about the
death of Jesus and that if we make room for all their diverse
approaches and ask how they relate to one another, we shall not
be deceived. At any rate it is in that faith that we press on with
our task.

If then we are to be faithful to the whole gospel record we have
to reckon with a dying Jesus who in his suffering and abandon-

ment is compassionate and gracious, both praying for and himself imparting a forgiveness that his death somehow makes possible. In that desolation and compassion he is bringing to its final fulfilment God's judging and saving purpose for his people and his world.

In each of the gospels one of these aspects is highlighted, but the other two are clearly implied. Mark's only reason for describing the desolation of Jesus is that it makes possible the restored access to God symbolised by the torn curtain of the temple and the confession of the centurion, the forerunner of the triumphs to come. Jesus' prayer for forgiveness is poignant and remarkable because it is offered in the midst of having the nails hammered through his hands and his feet. It is in the context of shared suffering that he wins his victory with the lost man beside him. For John the paradox is extreme; only from the thirsty man can there come redeeming blood and the river of living water; only the man who is at the end of his own life can inaugurate the life of the age to come. We are not to smooth over the differences and even the tensions among the gospel accounts, but we are not to exaggerate them either. Unless the cross were as agonising as Mark shows it, as effective as Luke shows it, and as ultimate and triumphant as John shows it, it could not be the central point in the gospels or fulfil its function in the faith that Christians confess.

In laying the biblical basis of our confession we have started with the gospel narratives of the crucifixion because they bring us as near as we can get to the event and the man who is our chief concern. It is that man and that event that are normative for all the later explanations that are offered of him and of it in the other New Testament writings and the atonement theology of the Church that flows from them.

His Life, His Cross, His Resurrection

But of course what happened that day on Calvary does not stand alone; it is the crowning completion of what goes before it and the basis of what comes after it and can be understood only in that double context. The gospels are written in the light of the fact that the crucified is risen and that God has said the enacted Yes of resurrection to all that Jesus did and offered from the cross. It is the resurrection that shows that Jesus of Nazareth is not just another failed Messiah. Without the resurrection, even if his vision and the way of salvation that he offered were different and indeed unique in their gracious magnificence, these wonderful promises would be as dead as he was when they took him down from the cross. Paul has no doubts about it; a cross without a resurrection is a crushing and disillusioning disaster: 'If Christ has not been raised, our preaching is useless and so is your faith' (1 Cor. 15:14). Only if the crucified is living and reigning does his suffering have meaning, is his forgiveness operative and his final victory won. His resurrection follows his death but his life and ministry precede it and the clues to what he dies for are to be found in the deeds and words that show us what he lived for. The controlling purposes and relationships of his life are also the controlling purposes and relationships of his death. To understand something of how Jesus approached his death and what he set himself to achieve by it, we have to look not just at the particular passages in which he speaks of it, often very enigmatically, but at the great concerns that dominated his ministry and the relationships with his Father and with his people in the service of which these concerns were pursued.

Jesus' Understanding of His Death

1. The Cross and the Baptism

John in the Jordan expresses these relationships at the very start of his ministry in his Baptism. This is one of the foundational acts of redemption, referred to in all four gospels although not always given its proper significance in the theological and liturgical tradition of the Churches of the West. Here Jesus is acknowledged as the Son who stands in unique relationship with his Father and who is anointed with the Holy Spirit for his messianic and more than messianic vocation: 'When all the people were being baptised, Jesus was baptised too. And as he was praying, heaven was opened and the Holy Spirit descended on him in bodily form like a dove. And a voice came from heaven: "You are my Son, whom I love; with you I am well pleased'"(Luke 3:21–2). It is in that relationship to *Abba* that Jesus lives and moves from the beginning of his life to the end. Everything that he says and does is done in loving and spontaneous attentiveness and obedience to his heavenly Father, and his death is the ultimate expression of that obedience as the synoptic accounts of his prayer in Gethsemane make clear: "'*Abba*, Father," he said, "everything is possible for you. Take this cup from me. Yet not what I will, but what you will"' (Mark 14:36). Jesus' death on the cross is to be seen as the culminating act of his obedience to his Father.

Furthermore, his Jordan baptism shows that his obedience to his Father leads him into identification with those who were disobedient to his Father. John's baptism was a baptism of repentance for those in Israel who had ceased to be authentic Israel, because they had broken their covenant with Israel's God. Why then was Jesus baptised? In this very story he is acknowledged as the anointed son with whom the Father is well pleased, so that he of all Israel has least need to repent. According to Matthew, John the Baptist, aware of the inappropriateness of this candidate for baptism, raised this very question and received what at that time could only be a rather unilluminating answer: 'Then Jesus came from Galilee to the Jordan to be baptised by John. But John tried to deter him, saying, "I need to be baptised by you, and do you come to me?" Jesus replied, "Let it be so now; it is proper for us to do this to fulfil all righteousness." Then John consented' (Matt. 3:13–15).

In the light of all that followed we can translate 'Fulfil all righteousness' as meaning 'Do all that needs to be done to bring God's people back into right relationship with him.' Jesus does that by identifying himself with them, in a baptism of repentance, where the repentance is not personal for himself but representative for them. We may therefore say that in his baptism Jesus is inaugurated into a ministry in which he is anointed to be the representative of God in his relationship with his estranged people and the representative of his estranged people in setting right their relationship with God. What Jesus does at the cross is the culmination of that double representation that starts with his baptism.

2. The Cross and the Kingdom

The dominating theme of that ministry is from the very start the coming of God's kingdom: 'After John was put in prison, Jesus went into Galilee, proclaiming the good news of God. "The time has come," he said. "The kingdom of God is near. Repent and believe the good news!"' (Mark 1:14–15). With the coming of Jesus, God's time, his *kairos*, his long-awaited moment of fulfilment for Israel, has arrived. It is the time when all his ancient promises will begin to be kept and when his ultimate purposes for his people will become effective. His kingdom is the community in which that is to happen, a new social order in which people are in right relationship with God and with one another, where sins are forgiven, where outcasts are restored, the sick in body healed and those held in spiritual oppression set free. The ministry of Jesus is to vanquish the human, the corporate, the spiritual forces that stand in the way of the kingdom to 'bind the strong man' (Mark 3:27), so that all those who have been captives in his prison may be set free.

The words and works of Jesus are directed towards the establishment of this kingdom, not in some inner or heavenly realm but in the flesh and blood reality of Israel's history which is reaching its final crisis and culmination in him. The good news of the gospel is that this has started to happen and the call of the gospel is for people to turn from all their other concerns and orientate themselves wholly to the kingdom and the king. King and kingdom are inseparable. The arrival of the kingdom is the arrival of Jesus, to enter the kingdom is to follow Jesus. He is not only the prophet who proclaims it but the one who, in his union with the Father, incarnates the kingdom and makes himself responsible for its coming and opens it to others, often to the people one would least expect to find there.

The coming of the kingdom is the radical fulfilment of Israel's election. Now it becomes clear how the promise to Abraham – that in his seed all the families of the earth will be blessed (Gen.12:3) – will be kept. 'So I say to you that many will come from the east and the west, and will take their places at the feast with Abraham, Isaac and Jacob in the kingdom of heaven' (Matt. 8:11). The coming of the kingdom will prove to be of universal significance. It will burst out of the bounds of Israelite exclusivism and gather to itself the Gentile world. But it becomes clear from the start that this coming of the kingdom is going to be opposed. The ministry of Jesus is from first to last the story of growing opposition to the kingdom and the king and of the realisation by Jesus that the work of its establishment can be achieved only by his suffering and dying: 'From that time on Jesus began to explain to his disciples that he must go to Jerusalem and suffer many things at the hands of the elders, chief priests and teachers of the law, and that he must be killed and on the third day be raised to life' (Matt. 16:21).

It is as the king coming to establish the kingdom that Jesus stages his Palm Sunday entrance into Jerusalem. He comes as a king who is subversive of all the powers that be which confront him. He challenges zealot nationalism and temple religion in both its sadducean and pharasaic forms. The kingdom comes not when Rome is vanquished or the law is kept but when the king on his cross acts as a representative of God in relation to his people and as a representative of Israel, albeit a rejected one, in relation to their God. It is entirely in keeping with the whole mission of Jesus that on the cross he should be placarded as Jesus of Nazareth, king of the Jews. This is the culminating act in the coming of the kingdom.

3. The Cross and Gethsemane

At the same time it is an infinitely costly act from which Jesus in the vulnerability of his humanity shrinks and even in Gethsemane prays to be rescued. The contrast is often drawn between the serenity of Socrates as he waits for the hemlock to work and the shrinking of Jesus from the cup that was to be put in his hand. For Socrates death was the escape of the soul from the shackles of the body to an assured immortality; for Jesus the cross was banishment into the dark and dreadful realm of the absence and the wrath of God. As von Balthasar reminds us, the cup in Gethsemane 'is not a matter of just any suffering, but the Old Testament, and also apocalyptic, cup of the divine anger which the sinner must drain (Isaiah 51:17 and 22; Jeremiah 15:15; Ezekiel 23:31ff; Psalm 75:9, etc.).'[6] This is the cup that in his obedience the Son willingly accepts from the hand of the Father, because the taking of this cup is the door to the kingdom for all on whose

behalf he drinks it. The cross is the culmination of the obedience
that the coming of the kingdom entails.

4. The Cross and the Last Supper

All these themes that emerge from the ministry of Jesus are gathered up in the event that most discloses his mind about his death,
namely the Last Supper in the upper room. The four accounts of
that event in the three synoptics and in 1 Corinthians (11:11–26)
differ in detail but the central understanding of what is going on
is common to them all. The claim of the Last Supper narrative to
go back to Jesus himself and to reflect in essentials his intentions
as he went to his death are very strong indeed. If we are not in
touch with the historical Jesus at this point, we must despair of
ever finding him at all.

At this point, however, we have every reason for confidence.
Jeremias points out that the Pauline account of the Lord's Supper
must go back to within a decade of the event itself and that there
are reasons for believing that the Markan account is even earlier.
He concludes:

> That in the remaining space of at most a decade after the
> death of Jesus the eucharistic rite should have been freely
> created, and the account of the Lord's Supper invented as an
> aetiological legend, is as much incapable of proof as it is
> improbable. It is even improbable that in the first decade
> after the death of Jesus the traditions should be in any essen-
> tials obscured; against that we have to set the complete
> unanimity in content of the mutually independent reports of
> Mark and Paul which come from different sections of the
> Church.[7]

In the discussion of these passages there is endless and detailed
controversy about almost every word of every verse, so that
sometimes one cannot see the wood for the twigs, let alone the
trees. For our purposes it will be enough to know that there is a
good consensus of mainline New Testament scholarship to
support the understanding of the Last Supper to which we now
turn.

New Passover, New Covenant, New Humanity

(a) The Last Supper as Passover Meal

We should notice first of all that this is, according to the three synoptics, a Passover meal in the course of which Jesus replaces the Passover liturgy with a new one of his own, in which he offers to the disciples his body and his blood, that is, himself and his life, by means of bread and wine. The Exodus from Egypt was the defining moment in which Israel came to know its God and its liberation. Jesus is telling his disciples that a new and ultimate defining and liberating moment has arrived. Through his death on the cross his people will come to know their God in a new way and will be rescued from a deeper and more fundamental captivity to the powers of evil than their ancestors in Egypt ever knew.

Furthermore as the blood of a lamb on their lintels marked the deliverance from death in Egypt into freedom with Yahweh, so this great liberation will be achieved 'through my blood of the covenant which is poured out for many' (Mark 14:24). Through what he does and suffers, they will enter into a new covenant, a new relationship, with God. Once again, as at his baptism, Jesus sees himself as acting and suffering on behalf of many others, giving to them a deliverance from the past and an entrance into the future that they had no part in achieving. That word at the Supper coheres with the other word in Mark with its strong resonance of the suffering servant of Isaiah 53: 'For even the Son of Man did not come to be served, but to serve, and to give his life as a ransom for many' (Mark 10:45). In that verse he speaks of the costly self-giving that is needed to set his people free, at the supper he offers himself to them, and on the cross he pays the price of their freedom.

(b) Pardon for Many

Matthew in his version of the Last Supper expands the Markan word over the cup so that the blood of the covenant is 'poured out for many for the forgiveness of sins' (Matt. 26:28) making explicit what is implicit in Mark's version. This is axiomatic for all later New Testament thinking about the cross: that on the cross

Jesus who had identified himself with the sinners in his baptism is here on the cross offering himself on their behalf to deliver them from the consequences of past sin and to break its power to dominate the future. This is the sin offering, the sacrifice that takes away sin.

What Jesus does, he does 'for many', a well recognised Semitic idiom meaning 'for all'. Liberation from sin is not a need peculiar to Israel, it is universal and the action and passion of Jesus on the cross is in the supper offered 'to many – to all'.

(c) The New Covenant

In the doing of it he establishes a covenant, in the Pauline version in 1 Corinthians 'the new covenant (*kaine diatheke*) in my blood' (1 Cor. 11:25). The God of Israel is a God who enters into a covenant relationship with his people and a central prophetic hope, typically expressed by Jeremiah, was that in the last days that covenant would be renewed and fulfilled:

> 'The time is coming,' declares the LORD, 'when I will make a new covenant with the house of Israel and with the house of Judah. It will not be like the covenant I made with their forefathers when I took them by the hand to lead them out of Egypt, because they broke my covenant, though I was a husband to them,' declares the LORD. 'This is the covenant that I will make with the house of Israel after that time,' declares the LORD. 'I will put my law in their minds and write in on their hearts. I will be their God, and they will be my people. No longer will a man teach his neighbour, or a man his brother, saying, "Know the LORD," because they will all know me, from the least of them to the greatest,' declares the LORD. 'For I will forgive their wickedness and will remember their sins no more.' (Jer. 31:31–4)

The new covenant that Jeremiah prophesies about and that Jesus inaugurates is in the first place 'with the house of Israel'. The intention of the cross as revealed in the Lord's Supper is not with individuals in isolation but with the whole people of God as a concrete social entity in its created time and place. The forgiveness that is promised is a renewal of Israel's relationship with its

God, its return from the exile of sin into the kingdom in which people know how to love God and how to love one another. At the cross we have not to do with individual spirituality or inward piety but with God's act in world history to renew his creation and human society in the midst of it.

A covenant has two parties to it as the Jeremiah passage makes clear. By it God becomes the God of his people, and his people become the people of their God. The people of Israel have failed to fulfil their side of that covenant. 'They broke my covenant.' But now Jesus comes fulfilling a double role of representation in regard to that covenant. He represents God in his reaction to this covenant-breaking people and he represents the people in his keeping of the covenant on their behalf, dealing with the consequences of their unfaithfulness and replacing it with his own faithfulness to it with the result that their iniquity is pardoned and their sin remembered no more.

This covenant is a social covenant with a whole people but it is one that is to be internalised by every member of the people who belong to it. 'They will all know me from the least to the greatest.' Only Jesus dies on the cross, only his body is broken and his blood shed, but that body and that blood, his very self and his life, are to be appropriated by and internalised in all who belong to him. The result of the cross is the personal and corporate union of the people with the crucified and risen Lord. That is present in the supper by the command to take and eat the bread and to drink of the cup. We are to feed on the body and blood, the self and the life of Jesus who died and rose for us.

(d) The Gift of a New Humanity

His gift in body and blood, the basic constituents of our humanity, the old sinful humanity that is to be taken to death on the cross and the new humanity that is to rise at Easter, is a result of what has been done on the cross. The death of Jesus is the birth of the new humanity, the death of the first Adam that he may be replaced by the last Adam, as Pauline atonement theology will later express it. That will be a major theme of this book and it is one that has its roots here in the Last Supper narrative. G. B. Caird commenting on the eucharistic discourse in John 6, which almost certainly has the Lord's Supper in mind, says:

At this point therefore [John 6.32] Jesus declares, 'Unless you eat the flesh of the Son of Man and drink his blood, you have no life in you.' Here we cannot improve on Westcott's understanding that 'by the "flesh" in this narrower sense we must understand the virtue of Christ's humanity as living for us, and by the "blood" the virtue of his humanity as subject to death.' The believer must be made partaker of both. The Son of Man lived for us and died for us, and communicates to us the effects of his life and death as the perfect human being. Without this communication of Christ men and women can have 'no life in themselves'.[8]

It is in the setting of such ultimate issues about humanity's relationship to God that, according to the enacted witness of the Last Supper, Jesus goes to his death. We have expounded it sufficiently to show that there is a clear continuity from Jesus' own mission and his understanding of how his death belonged to that mission and the atonement theology of the rest of the New Testament and of the later tradition that is derived from it. I have tried to expound it in a way that brings that continuity to light, so that we know, as we go on to the many questions that it raises, that they have their root in the way Jesus saw and approached his own death. We may fittingly end this chapter and in particular our exposition of the Last Supper narratives with the words of N. T. Wright whose own work has been in the background of my recent thinking on these matters.

When we add the words, even in outline, to the action, there should be no doubt but that Jesus intended to say, with all the power of symbolic drama and narrative, that he was shortly to die, and that his death was to be seen within the larger story of YHWH's redemption of Israel. More specifically, he intended to say that his death was to be seen as the central and climactic moment towards which that story had been moving and for which the events of the exodus were the crucial and determinative backdrop; and that those who shared the meal, not only then but subsequently were the people of the renewed covenant, the people who received 'the forgiveness of sins', that is, the end of exile. Grouped as they were around him, they constituted the true eschatological Israel.[9]

3

One Cross – Theodicy or Atonement?

Now that we have looked at the understanding of the cross that is implicit in the passion narratives of the gospels, the obvious next step is to turn our attention to the rest of the New Testament. There the interpretative framework within which the evangelists invite us to approach the cross is modified and expanded, so that it becomes more explicit, more universal and perhaps even more systematic in the letters of Paul, of Peter and of the anonymous writer to the Hebrews. These writings are normative for every doctrine of atonement that has emerged in the later life of the Church.

Before, however, we turn to that central and indispensable task, we are confronted by a difficulty that, if not unique to our own age and culture, is nevertheless characteristic of them. If this difficulty is not addressed, it could distance us from the presuppositions of the New Testament writers and make it hard for us to hear and appreciate the central thing that they want to say to us about the atoning death of Jesus.

The Sin Problem and Modern Culture

These writers, like the evangelists before them, present the message of the cross in quite distinctive ways, which we shall look at later, but common to them all, as indeed to the four evangelists, is the conviction that on the cross God in Christ was dealing with the central problem of human life. This is summed up in the word 'sin' understood as a radical and rebellious alienation from God, expressing itself in a multitude of ways in different people. For all of them sin, if not dealt with, was totally destructive of our relationships with God, with one another and with the world and would lead to the final destructiveness of death. As Paul puts it to the Romans: 'The wages of sin is death' (Rom. 6:23). The gospel was good news precisely because, through the death of Christ, God had dealt decisively with the sin problem and delivered us from that death which was the deserved consequence of sin, into a life which is the undeserved gift of God made available to us through the crucified Jesus: 'For the wages of sin is death, but the gift of God is eternal life in Christ Jesus our Lord' (Rom. 6:23).

This understanding of the work of Jesus culminating in his death as God's answer to human sin is clearly no later invention of the apostolic Church. It is, as we have seen, worked deeply into the gospel narratives all the way from Jesus' identification with sinners in his Jordan baptism to Matthew's report of his word over the cup at the Last Supper: 'This is my blood of the new covenant which is shed for you and for many for the remission of sins.' For Luke the cross is understood as Jesus' enacted prayer for the forgiveness of his crucifiers and as the gift of that forgiveness to the criminal who turns to him from the other cross. In John's gospel from the beginning the Baptist witnesses to Jesus: 'Behold the Lamb of God who takes away the sins of the world' (John 1:35).

That is how it has been seen down the Christian centuries and certainly at the time of the Reformation from which most of our official theological and liturgical approaches to the cross derive. The shared starting point of Martin Luther and the pardoners who were selling indulgences to fund the building of St Peter's in Rome, was that we were sinners under the judgement of a holy God and our greatest need in time and eternity was for that sin to be dealt with and taken away. They both addressed that problem, although they gave fundamentally different and incompatible answers to it, and that very fact gave them a point of contact with the New Testament gospel, which, as we shall see, is not nearly as accessible to us. It was natural for the Christians of the sixteenth century and their successors to see themselves, with Cranmer, as those who 'acknowledge and bewail our manifold sins and wickedness, which we . . .most grievously have committed by thought word and deed against thy Divine Majesty, provoking most justly thy wrath and indignation against us' and to cry for God's mercy to be released from that intolerable burden of guilt and to be forgiven all that is past for the sake of Jesus Christ.[1]

Such a prayer does not come naturally to the lips of modern worshippers and the confessions of sin in modern liturgies are much more muted in comparison with their Reformation predecessors. For the truth is that modern people are not in the same way worried about their sins and even less about a negative divine reaction to them. The result is that the New Testament claim that the cross is the unique and universal solution to the sin problem no longer engages us in an immediate way. We are not so interested in the remedy because we are no longer sure that we are suffering from the disease.

In a recent article Professor Mary Gray asks. 'Is sinfulness still an accepted category in our society for either the religious believer or non-believer?' and she goes on to report that when the University of Louvain in Belgium 'surveyed the attitudes on sin and guilt of European Christians in 1985, forty per cent of those interviewed *admitted that they had never experienced any feelings of regret about their actions.'*[2]

Such statistics take on flesh and blood in pastoral experience. It is only a year or two ago since I conducted a cremation service for the elderly mother of a family till then quite unknown to me, but whom I soon discovered to be deeply divided by unreconciled quarrels and unresolved disputes. As I entered the crematorium chapel I was greeted by the raucous voice of Edith Piaf singing *Je ne regrette rien* which, in its recorded implacability, soon drowned out and indeed silenced the gospel sentences with which the funeral service starts. Which things are parables; when people think they have nothing to regret the gospel of the cross cannot get a hearing! As Jesus put it ironically long ago: 'It is not the healthy who need a doctor, but the sick . . .'(Matt. 9:12).

Such instances are no doubt extreme, but they highlight the way that many contemporary people perceive themselves and their situation, and, if we are honest, because we are people of our time, we Christians also find it hard most of the time to get too concerned about our sins or the remedies that will free us from them.

Not Villains but Victims

Nowadays we tend to see ourselves as the passive victims of evil
and destructive forces over which we have no control, rather than
as the active agents of evil who can be held responsible for what
we do. We have been taught to understand our actions and our
attitudes in terms of the psychological forces that condition us
rather than in terms of the moral decisions that define us. We are
as we are and we do as we do because we are the victims of the
genes we have inherited, the parents who have nurtured us,
the society that has shaped us or the inner drives that impel
us. While these insights have taught us much about *why* we
behave as we do, they tend to undermine our sense of responsibility in the face of wrong.

To offer such an unqualified description of contemporary attitudes is of course to over-simplify to the point of caricature, but
even a caricature can have its uses if it helps us to recognise
some of the dominant factors in a much more complex situation.
Furthermore, to say that we often judge ourselves to be victims
rather than sinners is to say nothing at all about the validity of
that judgement. As we shall soon see, the debate about when and
to what degree we are passive victims or responsible agents is
one that rages in many different contexts in our day.

Two Contrasting Approaches to the Cross

The point that I want to make in connection with our subject is
that those who see themselves as the victims of evil will look at
the cross of Jesus with very different eyes from those who see
themselves as the responsible agents of evil. If we number ourselves with the evil-doers, we shall be open to and concerned
about questions of forgiveness, atonement and the restoration of
right relationships with a Holy God that have been the traditional
preoccupations of Christian atonement theology from the New
Testament onwards.

If on the other hand we number ourselves with the hapless
victims of evil forces, we shall want to know why these things
have been allowed to happen to us and by what means we can be
set free from the inner and outer things that dominate and

oppress us. We shall ask how the occurrence of such things is consistent with the Christian claim that the God in ultimate control of them all is the God and Father of our Lord Jesus Christ who has revealed to us his unlimited power and his unconditional love. When they turn theologians, sinners want to know how they can be justified before God, but victims want to know how God can justify himself to them. *So is it bad/ be like Job? inappropriate to*

The Cross as Theodicy

It is therefore perhaps not surprising that in a society of victims crying for justice and vindication, the old theologies of atonement should have lost much of their impact and their plausibility. They can be written off as attempts to answer questions that people are no longer asking. It is equally understandable that to fill the empty space and to regain relevance for its gospel the Church should have evolved a relatively new and very powerful theology of the cross. This theology stresses the death of Christ as the supreme instance and symbol of God's solidarity with innocent victims in their suffering, to the point that he himself in his Son asks the questions that all innocent victims ask: 'My God, my God, why have you forsaken me?'

If Gustav Aulén were to rewrite his classic book, *Christus Victor*, nowadays, he would need to recognise a fourth alongside the three types of Atonement theory that he identified fifty years ago. To the Classical, Latin and Subjective Theories that he described then, he would need to add the Theodicy or Suffering God theory that has been emerging all this century, but more formally and systematically in the theology of the last twenty or thirty years. This fourth type differs from the other three because they are all attempts to understand how on the cross God in Christ was reconciling us to himself. The new theory on the other hand is focused not on atonement but on theodicy. In other words its concern is not to show how humanity can be justified before God in the face of human sin, but rather how God can be justified to humanity in the face of human suffering.

The two approaches to the cross that we have just described as atonement and theodicy can easily be presented as mutually exclusive alternatives. If the chief concern of a theory of atonement is with how we can be made acceptable to God, the chief concern of theodicy is with how God can be made acceptable to us.

How can the God and Father of our Lord Jesus Christ who is revealed in the gospel as creating and recreating love be defended against the charge that he has made and maintains the kind of world in which meaningless and destructive suffering of all kinds abounds and is inflicted in a way that is totally arbitrary and that has no regard for any norm of justice? That is the theodicy question and it is one that can still rouse much interest and endless debate in our culture.

In contrast the atonement question that so exercised Paul, Luther and Wesley in their very different situations often seems remote and irrelevant to us. Outside and often even inside the churches, not many people have much vital interest in asking how sinful people who have turned from the living God to become their own gods and their own arbiters of what is good and evil, can be brought back into right relation with such a God. Yet that is the question that all views of atonement, whether Classical, Latin or Subjective, have raised and tried to answer.

To put the contrast between the two approaches at its starkest, the mainline Christian tradition has maintained that it is we who need to be forgiven for the way we have treated God, whereas the new approach wonders if it might not be God that needs to be forgiven for the way he has treated us. The theodicy question is man-centred in that it requires God to justify himself to us; the atonement question is God-centred in that it requires us to justify ourselves to God.

My purpose in this chapter is to ask how the new approach relates to the old. Are they alternatives so that to choose one is to reject the other, is it theodicy or atonement? If instead of being presented as an alternative to the old approach, the new were to be seen as complementary to it, might not the resulting integration give us a more comprehensive grasp of what God was doing when Jesus died on Calvary and rose again at Easter?

The Poets of the Trenches

Before we can answer such questions we need to look sympathetically at how the theodicy approach to the cross has in fact arisen in response to the suffering victims of the twentieth century. Its characteristic notes are already being sounded in the poetry that emerged from the slaughter of the First World War trenches. The characteristic response of poets to the horrors of war has hardly changed since Euripides, yet one or two of the poets of the First World War were able to find comfort in the identification of the crucified Jesus with them as the fellow-victim of cruel and undeserved suffering. So Isaac Rosenberg,

> Red fangs have torn
> His face,
> God's blood is shed.
> He mourns from his lone place,
> His children dead.[3]

During the 1914–18 War that prince of theologians P. T. Forsyth took up the same theme in a more formal way in a now nearly forgotten book, *The Justification of God*. In a key statement he said: 'Christ is the theodicy of God and the justifier both of God and the ungodly. The supreme theodicy is atonement.'[4] In putting it that way, Forsyth is on the one hand giving priority to the question of atonement over the question of theodicy, but on the other is suggesting that if we look into the heart of what God has done to justify us to himself we shall also see how, in so doing, he has justified himself to us. His main thrust is so similar to my own that his last sentence could almost stand as a motto text for this whole chapter: 'The supreme theodicy is atonement.' The two approaches belong together.

Moltmann and the Crucified God

For the systematic working out of these insights we have however to wait until after the Second World War, for those German theologians whose most accessible representative is Jürgen Moltmann in *The Crucified God*, first published in English in 1973. As the poetry was a response to the carnage of the First World War, so Moltmann's theology of the cross is a response to the atrocities of the Nazi period in general and to the Jewish holocaust in particular.

The question with which Moltmann approaches the cross is, post-Auschwitz what can a Christian theologian say about God? He quotes the well known account of E. Wiesel, a Jewish survivor of Auschwitz, who tells us how he saw a hanged Jewish youth taking half an hour to die in torment, and a fellow prisoner asked him, Where is God now? Wiesel goes on: 'And I heard a voice in myself answer, "Where is he? He is here, hanging there on the gallows."'[5] Wiesel himself has struggled since that day with the ambiguity of that answer. Did it mean that God was present in the agony, or did it mean that the agony made faith in the presence and reality of God for ever impossible?

Father and Son at the Cross

For Moltmann it is precisely at this point that the cross of Jesus becomes relevant. His whole book is in fact an extended Christian and Trinitarian exposition of that phrase, God on the gallows. It is Trinitarian because on the cross God the Son enters into the ultimate god-forsakenness of being abandoned by his Father to his suffering, so that he can identify with us in the despairing desolation of our own suffering and death. On Calvary the Son enters completely into the realm of destruction and death to seek out and rescue all the victims of suffering and death. The Father mourns for him as he suffers, but into the world of suffering and death he brings and releases the Spirit of life, makes a way through suffering to healing, through abandonment to restored relationship, through death to resurrection.

God in Christ, says Moltmann, 'humbles himself and takes upon himself the eternal death of the godless and the God-forsaken, so that all the godless and the God-forsaken can experience communion with him.'[6]

God in Auschwitz and Auschwitz in the crucified God – that is the basis for a real hope that both embraces and overcomes the world, and the ground for a love that is stronger than death and can sustain death. It is the ground for living with the terror of history and the end of history, and nevertheless remaining in love and meeting what comes in openness for God's future. It is the ground for living and bearing guilt and sorrow for the future of man with God.[7]

Even so short a summary lets us recognise that here we have a theology of the cross that addresses our contemporary situation with great relevance and power and there is that in all of us that responds to it with great warmth. It is a theology that situates itself well within the mainstream of the Christian tradition, because it also depends upon the high Christology embodied in its title, *The Crucified God*. For Moltmann's model to work, he who hangs on the cross must be 'very God of very God, of one being with the Father'.

Equally Moltmann's model requires a Trinitarian doctrine of God and indeed a major part of his achievement, as we have already seen in the first chapter, is to rescue the doctrine of the Trinity from its metaphysical remoteness and seeming irrelevance. Moltmann shows that the cross makes sense only in the Trinitarian terms of the relationship between a forsaking Father and a forsaken Son both of whom belong to and express the divine life of God and his identification with his people.

It must however now be clear that the theology of the cross we have been outlining speaks in terms of theodicy rather than of atonement. It neither is nor claims to be a full blown explanation of why there should be suffering and death in a world created by the sort of God that is revealed to us in Christ. Nevertheless it is orientated to theodicy in the looser sense because it undertakes to show how God engages with the suffering and death in the world in such a way as to vindicate his own character of accepting and identifying love that suffers and dies with us and so opens the way to the life and joy that is his purpose for his whole creation. It is not a theodicy of the past that explains suffering, but a theodicy of the future, of eschatological hope that shows how Christ makes himself one with the godless and the god-forsaken in order that they may be one with him in the risen life of his kingdom. Like all our theologies Moltmann's is open to criticism both in general and in particular, but it finally and powerfully engages with the suffering of our own times.

The Theodicy Model and the Bible

It is however when we begin to ask how such an approach relates
to the witness of the New Testament scriptures that problems
begin to arise. It is not that the two contradict each other, but that
each puts in the foreground what the other allows to remain in
the background. For Moltmann all the emphasis falls on God's
self-vindication in the face of suffering, and the reconciliation of
sinners, though never denied, is never properly expounded or
integrated into what he says. Commenting on Jesus' question
when dying: 'My God, why . . .?' he says:

> Ever since the New Testament, Christian theology has
> evolved a whole series of answers, which wrung permanent
> significance out of Christ's death. He suffered vicariously for
> us. He died as an atoning sacrifice for our sins. All these
> answers of faith are certainly not wrong, but if we imagine
> them being offered as an answer to the dying Christ crying
> out for God, then we sense immediately how inappropriate
> they are.[8]

Moltmann's theodicy of the cross is in fact an exposition of that
one saying of Jesus, which allows him to relate the event of the
cross to the victims of Auschwitz and all the other victims of
human oppression and injustice. In assessing his interpretation
we need to remember that many other of its expositors has interpreted the same word in terms of atonement theory.[9] But even
granted the rightness of Moltmann's understanding, the word of
desolation is not the only clue to the meaning of the cross in the
passion narratives, to say nothing of the rest of the New Testament. The central thrust is always that the blood of Christ is shed
'for the forgiveness of sins'. Paul is the great expounder of the
New Testament theology of atonement, but he was far from alone
in so doing. Peter and the writer to the Hebrews do the same in
their own distinctive ways because they are all simply reflecting
on something that was central and essential to the whole of
primitive Christianity and that we have good reason to believe
goes back to Jesus himself. Paul himself testifies that he did not
invent it but received it: 'For what I received I passed on to you as
of first importance that Christ died *for our sins* according to the
scripture' (1 Cor. 15:3).

It will not do therefore, with Moltmann, to brush aside Christ's vicarious and atoning suffering and death as 'certainly not wrong' but somehow secondary to the theodicy approaches based on the word of desolation somewhat isolated from its context. The weakness of theodicy type theologies of the cross is not in what they affirm, but rather in their connivance with the prevailing culture in relativising the sin problem over against the suffering problem. The result of this is to make secondary what in the New Testament is clearly primary. We cannot be true to the gospel unless we also give full weight to its claim that the primary meaning of the death of Jesus is that through it we are delivered from our sins.

Nevertheless, granted that primary focus, it is also true that the New Testament gospel provides a better basis for Moltmann's approach than we have so far allowed. In the way it delivers its primary message that Christ died for our sins, the New Testament tradition also shows him to us as the innocent victim who made common cause with those who suffer injustices of every kind. It belongs to the heart of the gospel story to present the crucified Jesus as *both* the one who died for sinners *and* the oppressed victim who suffered in a way he had done nothing to deserve. It is in fact because he is innocent in his suffering and death that he can help others through them.

We might even say that in a central atonement verse like 2 Corinthians 5:21, Christ is presented to us as at the same time vicarious sinner and vicarious victim. The central statement of the verse is that 'God made him who had no sin to be sin for us.' On behalf of sinners he dealt radically with our sin by entering into the depth and destructiveness of the human situation and radically changed it by offering himself from the midst of it in love and obedience to his Father. The cross, which is the summation of our destructive self-assertion turned against him in crucifying violence, he makes the summation of self-offering to God on our behalf. Thus he brings in himself our humanity, which he shares in all its lostness, back into loving and obedient relationship with his Father. The old sinful humanity he takes down into death and replaces it, through sharing that death, with the new humanity that is reconciled to the Father and is raised up to life in his kingdom.

This, however, he did and indeed could only do, in Paul's words, as 'one who had no sin'. He could bear sin because he had

committed no sin, he could bring people into right relationship
with his Father because, throughout his life and death, he
remained in right relationship with that Father. The accusations
that are made against him are false accusations; the verdicts that
are reached against him by the courts of Israel and Rome are
unjust verdicts, the result of the malice of the priests and the
cowardice of Pilate. Luke's centurion at the cross pronounces
the just verdict when he says, 'Surely this was a righteous man'
(Luke 23:48), and on the third day God himself as the ultimate
judge quashes the verdicts of the lower courts; they said, 'He
deserves to die,' but his Father said, 'He deserves to live.'

Therefore, as the innocent victim of all that befalls him, Jesus is
in solidarity with all the victims who have suffered at the
oppressive and unjust hands of the perpetrators of evil. It is at
this point that Moltmann's theology of the cross makes contact
with the biblical understanding of Christ's death and resurrection. The biblical writers do not develop the implications of
Christ's victimisation by the powers of evil in the way that
Moltmann does, but they say enough to establish his relevance to
all who suffer at the hands of evil oppressors: the young Jew
hanging on Calvary *is* in a like situation to the other young
Jew dangling from the gallows at Auschwitz.

One of the New Testament passages that comes nearest to that
sort of approach is 1 Peter 2:20, which addresses those who suffer
not as sinners but as people who are victimised precisely because
they are doing good. He reminds them, with the help of the
Suffering Servant passage from Isaiah 53, that Christ was one
such, exhorts them to respond to their suffering in the way that
Jesus did, and to trust to the God who vindicated Jesus to vindicate them as well. 'To this [unjust suffering] you were called,
because Christ suffered for you, leaving you an example that you
should follow in his steps. He committed no sin and no deceit
was found in his mouth. When they hurled insults at him, he did
not retaliate: when he suffered he made no threats. Instead he
entrusted himself to him who judges justly' (2:21–3). To this we
could add the many passages in which Paul rejoices in the sufferings of which he has been the victim, because Christ has made a
way through unjust suffering to deliverance, healing and life.

We may then conclude that the theodicy-type theology of the
cross, although never the primary emphasis, has a better basis in
the New Testament than might at first sight appear. Jesus is first

and foremost the Saviour from our sins but, as such, he is also the sharer of our sufferings and the companion who identifies with all who count themselves god-forsaken in their sufferings. To them he offers the hope of a way through suffering and death to liberation and life.

It may be that the culture of our time with its experience of and preoccupation with unjust suffering and oppression enables us to focus on this aspect of the theology of the cross much more clearly than previous generations with their heavy accentuation of our sinfulness. It may even be that, in the post-Auschwitz situation in which he was writing, Moltmann was perhaps right for good apologetic and pastoral reasons to emphasise Jesus' empathy with our suffering by detaching it temporarily from traditional atonement-type theology of the cross. In so doing he has helped us to see that this kind of theodicy is an authentic aspect of any full Christian understanding of the work of Jesus. Its homiletic appeal, its pastoral relevance and its political implications show how significant and fruitful it can be in our contemporary situation. When I was trying to persuade reluctant and practically-minded Anglican ordinands of the importance and relevance of systematic theology, as soon as I introduced them to Moltmann, my task was as good as done!

Nevertheless these two approaches to the cross very much need to be reintegrated. We must develop a theology of the cross that has room for both atonement and theodicy. The latter must never be presented as some sort of modern alternative to the atonement-type approach, however immediately attractive it may be to our contemporaries. In his later book, *The Spirit of Life*, Moltmann himself is moving towards just such a reintegration. In a chapter entitled 'The Justifying Justice of God for the Perpetrators', he says: 'There is more in this [Christ's death on the cross] than Christ's *solidarity* with the accursed of the earth. In this is the divine atonement for sin, for injustice and for violence . . .He [God in Christ] moulds and alchemizes the pain of his love into atonement for the sinner. In this way God becomes the *God of sinners*.'[10] For every sufferer in war, in holocaust, in ethnic cleansing, there has been a sinner.

It is interesting to notice how in the passage we have just quoted from 1 Peter, Jesus is no sooner identified as the model of the innocent victim than he is also proclaimed as the Saviour from sin. The passage continues: 'He himself bore our sins in his body on the tree, so that we might die to sins and live for righteousness; by his wounds you have been healed' (2:24). The wounds inflicted on him as victim become the means by which he accomplishes our healing as Saviour.

On the biblical level Christ is both victim and reconciler, the one who justifies God to us by his sharing of our suffering, and the one who justified us to God by his atonement for our sin. Because the biblical testimony is the norm for all the theology that is based on it, the same integration must take place in the way that we confess the cross in the Church and to the world. In all that follows we have to expound the relevance of Calvary to both victims and villains; the passive sufferers and the active perpetrators of evil.

Both Villains and Victims

We may ask why Christ's one integrated work is relevant to what at first sight seem two quite distinct categories of people, the innocent victims and the guilty sinners. However, we need to ask whether the categories are as distinct as the question presupposes. The victims and the perpetrators of evil may turn out to be the same people. If our Reformation forebears saw themselves as sinners rather than victims and if we in our day see ourselves as victims rather than sinners, the truth may be that we are always both.

In the end there are no victims of evil who are themselves wholly innocent. Innocence is always relative rather than absolute. In particular situations we are indeed the passive victims of evils that we have had no part in bringing upon ourselves; they are due entirely to the malevolence of others or the accident of unfavourable circumstances. Nevertheless our reactions to the evils done to us are often far from innocent. We have all heard the relatives of victims of crime displaying a relentless and sometimes murderous hatred against the person they hold responsible, expressed everywhere in the contemporary rush to litigation, so that the attitudes on both sides are far distant from the kind of love that the Father reveals to us in his Son. Both parties to the deed, villain and victim alike, are shown to be sinners who by their action and their reaction are in contradiction to God's gracious purpose and plan.

In some early Liberation theology there was what amounted to a romanticising of the poor and the oppressed, which almost suggested that to be poor was to be good and to be oppressed was to be godly. It is however quite illegitimate to argue from the important biblical insight that God has a bias for the poor to its converse that the poor have a bias for God. We do not need to look further than Bosnia and Rwanda for proof that, when the victims become the victors, the old oppressed can quickly turn into the new oppressors and practice against their erstwhile exploiters the same cruel and vindictive outrages from which they themselves once suffered. In divorce legislation the notion of the 'innocent party' in a failed marriage has had be discarded as untenable, because although one party may have been the ostensible victim of the infidelity, cruelty or desertion of the other, when the situation is probed, it will be discovered that the 'victim' has a considerable share of responsibility for the way things have gone.

On the small scale and the personal level many of us can remember undeserved hurts and injustice done to us that made us aware not only of the bad intentions and actions of others towards us, but also of the dark and murky things in ourselves that our reaction to our wrongs revealed. We become adept at using the hurt done to us to justify our hostility to its perpetrator, and a bit of us delights in sophisticated campaigns of revenge. We want to hold on to the wrong rather than be reconciled to the wrongdoer because that would deprive us of the superior status of 'innocent' victim in which we find a perverted satisfaction. It is often when we are victims that we find that to our shame we are also villains and sometimes the beam in our own eye is a lot more destructive than the speck in our brother's, and we recognise often very belatedly that we have more to be forgiven than we have to forgive.

But it is equally true that if the victims are also villains, the villains are also victims. There is indeed a lively contemporary debate in our society about how much we are the one and how much the other. Every time there is an outbreak of violence in a housing estate, there will be arguments as to whether what happened was the inevitable result of the poor parenting, unemployment and social deprivation of those who have broken the law or whether they did what they did by conscious deliberate decision for which they can be held personally and totally responsible. The way that argument goes has obvious and important implications for penal policy, and the debate rages on.

In such a complicated situation it is unlikely that the truth will be found at either end of the spectrum. On the one hand people are not just the passive victims of the determinism of social forces that are quite outside their control. On the other hand an individualistic Pelagianism that thinks that the moral status of people and their actions can be judged out of relationship to all the influences that have shaped the environment in which a person has been shaped and formed is equally simplistic. The truth may well be that we are both victims and villains.

On the one hand the evil that we do does not have its origin in ourselves and our choices but comes from a context into which we have by no fault of our own been born, in which we are trapped and from which we cannot extricate ourselves. On the other hand that evil does not have its way in our attitudes and actions without our giving our consent to it, without our yielding to what is at first a temptation to which we have not consented, but becomes, in our yielding to it, something we have taken to ourselves and made our own, and for which therefore we have assumed responsibility.

Sin as Captivity

The trouble is that what we let in takes over. The single evil action easily becomes the fixed habit and can then become seated somewhere near the centre of our personality. This is accompanied by a dulling of conscience so that initial remorse dulls into easy toleration which in turn fades into a complacency that is no longer troubled by moral criticism either from conscience within or authority without. It is this dulling of conscience that Jesus is describing when he says: 'Light has come into the world, *but men loved darkness instead of light because their deeds were evil*' (John 3:19). Espoused evil destroys both our awareness of it and our resistance to it, so that at the cross the protagonists of Jewish religion and the defenders of Jewish law crucify love incarnate with only the dimmest awareness of what is involved in their own act. That may be why Jesus prays for them as people who are the victims of their own sinning and have to be regarded less with condemnation than with compassion: 'Father, forgive them, *because they do not know what they are doing.*' The greatest villains of the piece are also its greatest victims.

That is the situation that Paul describes in personal terms in Romans 7, whether as part of his Jewish experience of the past or his Christian experience of the present – a much debated point into which we need not enter here. As a sinner he is also a victim: 'For what I do is not the good I want to do; no, the evil I do not want to do – this I keep on doing. Now if I do what I do not want to do, it is no longer I who do it, but it is sin living in me that does it' (Rom. 7:19–20). By his sinful actions he has become the prisoner of a power from which he does not know how to be free; in his own words, 'the prisoner of the law of sin and death at work within my members' (7:23).

It is this awareness of his moral captivity to sin that turns his hope of rescue away from himself and his own efforts to Christ and what he has done for him: 'What a wretched man I am! Who will rescue me from this body of death? Thanks be to God – through Jesus Christ our Lord!' (Rom. 7:24–5). All Pelagian notions of self-rescue from the power of sin are shown to be superficial in their diagnosis and ineffective in their results. Such a Pelagianism is in the end unrealistic in its demands, cruel in its condemnation and rigorous in its punishments. We are not as responsible as it would make us. True we have freely aligned ourselves with the forces of evil that press in upon us, but, being admitted, they have taken over and we are incapable of getting ourselves out. Even as responsible sinners, we are helpless victims who can be rescued only by the compassion of him who came to seek and find us and do for us what we could not do for ourselves.

Original Sin

This dialectic relationship between the sin we commit and the sin that has victimised us is at the heart of the much-neglected doctrine of original sin. This finds its first formal expression in Paul's teaching in Romans 5 about our solidarity with Adam in his and

our sinning. We are each born into and surrounded by a fallen
humanity, deeply ingrained in its age-long rebellion against God.
We are therefore victims of a sinful situation far beyond our own
making, and yet at the same time *willing* victims, who have made
common cause with the race in its rebellion, taken personal
responsibility for our own Yes to its corporate No to God. The sin
around us is by our own act internalised within us and we have
responsibility for our own part in its continuance and perpet-
uation.

The doctrine of original sin is misunderstood if it is taken, as it
sometimes has been, as an *explanation* of the origin of sin; that
remains an insoluble mystery. What we have here is rather a
general description of the situation, which Paul describes in terms
of personal experience in Romans 7. We are both the perpetrators
and the victims of evil and we are to be taken equally seriously in
both capacities. We must not, as is the modern tendency, allow
the realisation that we are victims to exculpate us from responsibility for our actions: equally we must not allow the reality of our
responsibility to obscure the reality of our victimisation and
our helplessness. Determinism and Pelagianism will both fail to
sound the dark depths of the human predicament. Enticed by
false promises, we have freely joined others in the dark room
where evil is king, only to hear the door clanging behind us and
making the place a prison to which we have no key. It is by our
fault that we are captives, but it is beyond our capability to set
ourselves free.

It is to such a situation that the work of Christ in the cross
is offered as God's answer. However, before he deals with the
situation, Jesus on the cross first exposes it. The doctor who
comes to seek and to save the sinners offers a diagnosis before he
works a cure. Contemporary people, as we saw at the start of the
chapter, are often not aware that they have anything to regret
or repent; when they assess themselves or measure themselves
against the norms of the society they live in, they can easily reach
what is on the whole a very positive verdict.

It is when we are all measured by the love of Jesus that itself
reflects the love of the Father, from whom he came, that we
begin to see ourselves very differently. It is not that he accuses or
condemns us; we have his own word for it that he did not come
to do either. It is by being what he is and doing what he does, in
his life and supremely in his death, that he enables us to see

ourselves by contrast with him as we really are. It is in their reaction to him that disciples, churchmen, politicians, ordinary people show that they are not in the last resort the friends of God's love, but its crucifying enemies. In this way the priests of religion and the upholders of the Jewish law, the disciples who are pledged to loyalty, the Roman authorities with their reputation for upholding justice, the crowds who can be easily manipulated to bay for his blood – all are revealed as having nails and hammers in their hands.

It is the coming of God, the loving of God, the dying of God that shows us how far from God we really are. Most of all perhaps our religion and our morality are often elaborate defences against the realisation of the dark truth about ourselves and where we stand with God. What convicts people of sin is not the fulminations and accusations of the moral law, but the man on the cross who indeed loves the Lord his God with all his heart and soul and mind and strength and his neighbour as himself. In so doing he shows us how little we love either and are indeed the perpetrators and the victims of the sin that rejects him and nails him to the cross. The preaching of the past could often take the awareness of sin for granted; today we have to preach Christ crucified whose love convicts as it converts, reveals as it redeems, judges as it saves.

In this chapter we have seen that theodicy and atonement belong together; God's love in Christ makes common cause with sufferers in the same act in which it brings liberation to sinners. We are all in our different ways both the active agents as well as the passive victims of evil and Christ goes to the cross so that the villains who are the victims and the victims who are the villains might go free.

4

One Cross – The Decisive Deed

The title of this chapter outlines its main agenda which can be summed up in the two questions: 'What was the fundamental nature of the deed that Christ performed on the cross, and how was it decisive for the rest of us who, as we have seen, are both the victims and the agents of evil?'

We often speak of the passion of Christ but, if we are to be true to the New Testament witness, we have to see that his passion was also his action, his decisive deed. It was not simply a fate that befell him by the plotting and planning of his enemies, but something that he undertook, after much struggle (as the Gethsemane stories make clear) but deliberately, as the central act of his obedience to the Father. John is especially concerned to emphasise this. For him Jesus approaches the cross saying: 'No one takes it [my life] from me, but I lay it down of my own accord. I have authority to lay it down and authority to take it up again. This command I received from my Father' (John 10:18). In the same gospel he dies with the great cry *Tetelestai*, it is finished, it is perfectly accomplished. The cross is no tragedy passively endured, but an action deliberately undertaken and successfully completed. It therefore makes sense to ask what it meant for the man who chose it and for those on whose behalf it was chosen. This was indeed his deed.

Further, if we are going to be true to the biblical witness, we have to say that this was a decisive deed both for him and for those on whose behalf it was done. The word that the New Testament regularly uses to indicate the uniqueness and decisiveness of this deed is the Greek word *hapax*, 'once', or, even more strongly, *ephapax*, 'once and for all'. This book's title is in fact a translation of that word, and its main purpose is to expound the uniqueness and decisiveness of the deed done on the cross.

The Decisive Deed – in the New Testament

It is the word that Paul uses in exactly our context in Romans:
'The death he died, he died to sin *once for all* (*ephapax*), but the life
he lives, he lives to God' (Rom. 6:10). So also Peter: 'For Christ
died for sins once for all (*hapax*), the righteous for the unrighteous, to bring you to God' (1 Pet. 3:18). In the Letter to the
Hebrews the universal effectiveness and unrepeatability of the
death of Christ becomes a major theme in contrast to the often
repeated and never effective Old Testament temple sacrifices. So
Hebrews 7:27: 'Unlike the other high priests, he [Christ] does not
need to offer sacrifices day after day, first for his own sins, and
then for the sins of the people. He sacrificed for their sins once for
all (*ephapax*) when he offered himself.'

His death is decisive not just in relation to the sacrificial system
of the past but to all the sins of the future. If he had been like the
Aaronic high priests, 'Then Christ would have had to suffer
many times since the creation of the world. But now he has
appeared *once for all* (*ephapax*) at the end of the ages to do away
with sin by the sacrifice of himself.' Furthermore his one death
achieves perfect holiness for all who belong to him:

> We have been made holy through the sacrifice of the body of
> Jesus Christ *once for all* (*ephapax*). Day after day every priest
> stands and performs his religious duties; again and again he
> offers the same sacrifices, which can never take away sins.
> But when this priest had offered for all time one sacrifice for
> sins, he sat down at the right hand of God. Since that time he
> waits for his enemies to be made his footstool, because by
> one sacrifice he has made perfect for ever those who are
> being made holy. (Heb. 10:10–14)

Our perfection is not so much something still to be achieved in
us, still less by us, but rather something that has already been
achieved in and by him of which we have to take possession and
make our own.

Thus three of the central streams of New Testament reflection
on the cross, Paul, Peter, Hebrews are united in their insistence on
the completeness and distinctiveness of what Jesus did there. It
was one time for all times, it was the deed of one man that
transformed the whole situation for everybody else. We can

therefore claim some biblical justification for the *double entendre* of our title. What he did on the cross was not just once-and-for-all, it was 'once – and for ALL!'

It follows therefore that any theology of the cross that denies or diminishes the uniqueness and decisiveness of Calvary is seriously defective from a biblical point of view. The cross is far more than the revelation and manifestation at one point in human history of a grace and a love that operate in the same way at every point of human history.

It is of course true that God's love and grace are as eternal as he is himself and are therefore operative in different ways and to different degrees in all his dealings with all people everywhere. Nevertheless the Christian claim is that as God is present uniquely and decisively in the incarnation of his Son, so he acts finally and savingly in relation to our sin and suffering when that Son is crucified. God in his Son was on the cross for three hours on the first Good Friday. He had never been there before and he will never be there again. What he did there he had never done before and will never have to do again. Other people at all other times and places have to relate to what he did for them at a place where most of them have never been and at a time when most of them were not born. That is the clear implication of the *ephapax* with which the New Testament so clearly highlights the decisiveness of the cross.

The Cross is Decisive for God

What we have just been saying also implies that the cross, like the incarnation itself, is not only decisive for us but is also decisive for God. For him it marks a new and ultimate phase in his relationship with humanity. In Christ he became man and in Christ, to speak with Paul in the Philippians hymn, he 'made himself nothing, taking the very nature of a servant, being made in human likeness. And being found in appearance as a man, he humbled himself and became obedient to death – even death on a cross!' (Phil. 2:7–8). God in the heavenly glory of his love has ever been sensitive and responsive to the suffering of his creation, but only on Calvary has he known from the inside the physical pain, the mental agony, the spiritual desolation of death on the cross. Paul Fiddes who, to my mind, leaves much to be desired in his dealing with the decisiveness of the cross for us, is quite clear about its decisiveness for God:

> He is the sympathetic Creator who shares the lives of his creatures, experiencing the agony of all those who suffer and receiving their hurt as his own. This did not happen only at the cross, but happens continually as God identifies himself with the weak and the oppressed. However at the cross his being was drawn most closely into the pain and desolation of the victim because of the closest union between himself and this human Son, so that his universal sympathy is always grounded in this particular experience.[1]

On the cross God took upon himself the uttermost depths of human suffering and the most extreme consequences of human sin; he came there in Christ, although he did not stay there. The Philippians hymn does not end with the one who was in the form of God becoming obedient to death even death on a cross, but continues: 'Therefore God has highly exalted him and given him the name which is above every name.' But his exaltation is the exaltation of the crucified, and in all his later dealings with us, as Hebrews makes clear, he speaks and acts as the crucified and risen *Kurios*, who has been under the weight of our sufferings and our sins and is able to help us in them for that very reason.[2] In that way the cross is decisive for God.

The Cross is Decisive for Us

It follows that if it is decisive for God, it is also and all the more decisive for us. It must not be reduced simply to a specific historical revelation of a universal eternal truth. It is not only symbol and expression of the saving love of God: it is that love moving into eventful operation that in and by itself changes and transforms our relationship to God.

(a) The Denial of Decisiveness

One of the ways in which what P. T. Forsyth called the cruciality of the cross has been obscured is in that strand of atonement theology which is associated with the writings of Peter Abelard and which has found its contemporary champion in Paul Fiddes. For Abelard and Fiddes what Jesus did on the cross has value not so much in and for itself as for what it produces and enables in other people. The decisive happening does not take place on Calvary but in those whose repentance and conversion is enabled by what Christ did on Calvary. Expounding Abelard, Fiddes can say: 'Though atonement has been achieved potentially in the event of Christ, it only becomes *actual* in the present, as people make the victory of Christ their own.'[3]

That is a typical statement of the Arminian individualism which insists that my relationship to God depends on what has been done in me in the present rather than what has been done for me by Christ in the past. This view does indeed concede that my present condition is evoked and created by the influence of the past event upon me, but the determining factor is what has happened in me rather than that what was achieved by him. The cross yesterday has to have its potential realised by my response to it today.

(b) The Denial Criticised

(i) It Undermines Assurance

The implications of this become clearer when we see how Fiddes explains it in relation to penitence in his discussion of the forensic or legal model of atonement: 'The justice of God demands, and is satisfied by, the penitence of people down through the ages as they share in the penitence of Christ.'[4] And again: 'This legal model of atonement tells us not that he endures a penalty instead of us, but that he can create a penitence within us. Such penitence is expiating in that it wipes out sin by replacing an attitude of sinful rebellion with an attitude of home-coming.'[5]

My first reaction to that is one of personal horror! What the justice of God demands and is satisfied by is 'the penitence of people down the ages'. 'Such penitence is expiating.' My trust for my salvation is to be grounded in the present state of my personal response to God in penitence. Even though that penitence has been evoked and created by the crucified Christ, what counts with God, satisfies his justice, turns away his wrath and overcomes sin is my act now rather than his act then.

This is an invitation to morbid introspection, if ever there was one. If I look at myself and the quality and extent of my penitence, I shall be continually wondering if I have repented enough to satisfy the divine demand that is being made upon me, and, if I have any kind of honesty and integrity before the judgement of God, continually coming to the conclusion that I have in fact done neither. The more I become aware of his holiness, the less satisfied will I be with my own. This is certainly not the road to any of Christian assurance, rather a downhill highway to despair.

Such an existential protest may be thought sufficient in itself to question very radically Fiddes' position on this matter. It does however need to be backed up by objections of a more formally theological nature, and these are by no means lacking.

(ii) It is Inadequate to Biblical Teaching

To understand the work of Christ on the cross as having its value in its potential to enable our response to it, is to fail to do justice to the witness of the New Testament writers to its sufficiency and completeness. In 2 Corinthians 5:18 Paul speaks of how God 'reconciled us to himself through Christ'. The verb used is the aorist participle *katallaxantos* which speaks of a work already done and not of a potential for reconciliation still to be actualised. In the same chapter Paul does indeed go on to bid us be reconciled, but the relationship of our response to his deed is not be understood, with Fiddes, in a way that denies the cruciality of the cross and emphasises instead the decisiveness of our response to it. How that relationship is to be understood we must take up later, but it is much more a matter of our entering into something that was complete without us, than our actualising something that was merely potential without us. The language Paul uses in this passage shows that he could not have been thinking of it in that way.

The same point is made in Romans 5:10 where Paul describes how 'when we were God's enemies, we were reconciled [aorist verb again] to him through the death of his son.' The reconciling deed was done and done completely while, far from being returning penitents, we were rebellious enemies. Our penitence is indeed its intended consequence, but that penitence follows upon rather than itself constitutes the decisive transformation of our relationship with God.

(iii) It Rejects Representation

Fiddes speaks of the work of Jesus on the cross in terms of the causality that it exerts; the exemplary and empowering influence it has on those who are exposed to it. His death moves us to repentance, his great love for us moves us to a like love of himself and his Father. The cross works through the influence of one individual on all the other individuals who fall under his spell. In all this there is not a trace of the notion of Christ's representation of the rest of humanity, his acting on our behalf and even in our stead. In the writings of the New Testament Christ is regularly said to act *huper hemon*,[6] on our behalf and occasionally even *anti hemon*,[7] in our stead and we in turn are said to be *en Christo*, in Christ. The implications of this are spelled out in Paul's rich teaching of Christ as the *eschatos* Adam, the ultimate man who shares his new humanity with all who belong to him. These prepositions, the significance of which has been drawn out in the mainstream theology of the Church, are very different and much richer than the rather external influencing of the many by the one, envisaged by Fiddes.

(iv) It Confuses Justification and Sanctification

This approach involves a confusion of justification with sanctification that is closely related to the debates of the sixteenth century Reformers with their Roman Catholic opponents. For a certain kind of medieval Catholicism people come into right relationship to God, in the technical jargon, are 'justified', only when the grace of God has had its complete way with them and they reflect his holiness in their own, that is, are perfectly sanctified. It is not hard to see the similarities between such a view and that of Fiddes. For him also we have to reach that degree of penitence that satisfies God before we can be said to be in right relationship with him. In both cases, the grace and the penitence have their source in Christ's cross, but what counts is not what he did there but what sanctification it subsequently produces in us.

Against this the Reformers maintained, as we have been doing, that the ground of our justification was not anything at all in ourselves but solely in what Christ had done on our behalf and in our place. His unique self-offering on Calvary was, in the words of the *Book of Common Prayer*, 'a full perfect, and sufficient sacrifice, oblation and satisfaction, for the sins of the whole world', and our faith therefore was not in what has happened in us through him, but in what he has done for us there and then. His 'one oblation of himself once offered' alone had the fullness, the perfection and the sufficiency for us to have a confident and assured faith in its power to bring us back into right relationship with the Father. As Paul puts it in Romans: 'Therefore, since we have been justified through faith, we have peace with God through our Lord Jesus Christ' (Rom. 5:1).

None of this is of course to deny or even diminish either repentance or sanctification in their essential relationship to the cross; it is simply to define that relationship in a different way. The importance of our repentance does not have to do with either its quality or its completeness; it matters simply because, however tentative and imperfect, it is the act in which we turn from ourselves to Christ, we put our faith not in anything in ourselves, however good or bad, but solely in what he has done for us. We ask God not to look at us and our repentance but rather at Jesus and his offering and we ask to be accepted for his sake; not because we have repented so fully but because he has offered himself so completely. To anticipate what we shall be saying later, the great repentance, the great change of attitude, the great return of humanity to God was in the life and death of Jesus and our turning to Jesus matters only because it links us up with him and what he did for us at Calvary.

Furthermore the aim of his offering is our sanctification; we are accepted by God as we are in order that, through the crucified and risen Jesus, we should become what he wants us to be. As the Johannine Jesus says on the very brink of his passion: 'For them I sanctify myself, that they too may be truly sanctified' (John 17:19). Their ultimate sanctification is the longed for outcome of his sanctification at Calvary. But in order to be sanctified, they must first be accepted. *Their acceptance is the basis and not the result of their sanctification.* Because they are accepted as they are, they can be confident enough of their relationship with God and of his love for them to expose themselves to the demanding and life-changing processes that are involved in their becoming the people God wants them to be, so that his holiness is authentically reflected in theirs. If that relationship is reversed and our sanctification is seen as the condition of our acceptance, the whole process will be beset by constant anxiety and fear.

Such technical language must not be allowed to obscure a situation with which we are all familiar in our own family relationships. If acceptance of the child by the parent is conditional on the child's achievements, the overcoming of faults, the development of characteristics of which parents approve, academic or even sporting prowess of one kind or another, that child's relationship with his parents will be anxious and uncertain. If however the child is accepted and loved just as he or she is, good or bad, clever or stupid, achieving much or little, that love will give that child an ability to accept the disciplines the parents impose and the confidence to achieve some of the goals they desire.

So, on every level, acceptance precedes transformation and justification precedes sanctification. To reverse the relationship, as Fiddes at least by implication does, is not only biblically and theologically dubious but spiritually harmful as well.

For all these reasons, which have both theological and spiritual implications, we must reject Fiddes' whole approach to this matter. In the course of his book he has many good things to say about the work of Christ, but his whole interpretation is undermined by his attempt to move the decisive atoning moment from what Jesus did on Calvary to what we do when we are moved and empowered by him to our own acts of repentance and sanctification. To do that is to go too far with contemporary culture and its emphasis on the action of the free individual in the present, in a high degree of autonomy from the deeds of others in the past. Such a culture cannot but find it hard to come to terms with the decisiveness of the cross.

Up to this point we have been asserting that decisiveness against certain atonement theologies that have failed to do justice to it. Now we must look more closely at the biblical material and the way it has been interpreted in the later theology of the Church to see why the decisiveness of the cross is of such central importance and how we can expound and defend it today in a culture which, as we have seen, is unfriendly to it.

Decisiveness and the Classic Atonement Metaphors

We can start to do that by looking again at the classic metaphors that, first in the Bible, and then in the tradition have been used again and again to make sense of the gospel of the cross. From the first and down the Christian centuries, the cross has been seen as a victory over the powers of evil, as a sacrifice offered to remove sin, as a price paid to bring slaves into freedom, as an act of reconciliation that turns enemies into friends and as a means by which those who have been condemned by their sins are rendered acceptable in the judgement of a just and holy God.

Some of these metaphors are more immediately accessible to modern people than others. We know a lot more about winning battles, reconciling enemies and dispensing justice than we do about offering sacrifices and liberating slaves. None of the metaphors is complete in itself; each highlights certain aspects of the atoning work of Christ that are not so evident in the others.

Also, when they are applied to the cross, the metaphors are all given a paradoxical twist which reminds us that what Jesus did is defined as much by its unlikeness as its likeness to the other activities with which his action is being compared. The battle Christ fought and won is different from every other battle; the sacrifice Christ offered is different from every other kind of sacrifice. The way he releases slaves is quite different from all other acts of emancipation; the way he makes peace is quite distinct from all other peace negotiations and this judge pronounces an unheard of verdict and attains justice by making himself the victim of the people whose case he is trying.

These metaphors or models of atonement, which are all biblical in origin, have been used in very different ways down the centuries but, as John McIntyre points out:

> What we have witnessed in the history of the Church's thinking about the death of Christ has been the quite remarkable capacity on the part of such models to root themselves in a vast variety of heterogeneous cultures, and to find com-

prehensible expression in generations separated from one another sometimes by hundreds of years – and that fact is no less true today than it was 400 or 1500 years ago.[8]

That quotation may give us confidence to turn again to these metaphors and ask ourselves what each has to say about Christ's work on the cross in its distinctiveness and decisiveness. There will be some aspects of that work that are presented more prominently by particular metaphors and some that are common to them all. Our aim will be to distil from them as complete an account as we can of the great central issue that was engaged with and decisively settled when Jesus died for us all.

(a) The Battle Metaphor

We may look first at the victory in battle metaphor which has been very prominent in atonement theology in our own century, influenced as it has been by Aulén's classic, *Christus Victor*, whose title is eloquent of its emphasis. For Aulén Christ on the cross engages in battle all the hostile forces that hold man in bondage and in his resurrection celebrates his victory over them, so that in the power of his victory we also may overcome.

(i) Its Credentials

There is no doubt that this is one way in which the New Testament proclaims its gospel, although whether it is as central as Aulén claims is open to question, as Colin Gunton has pointed out.[9] Nevertheless we can think of such a passage as Colossians 2:15: 'And having disarmed the powers and authorities, he made a public spectacle of them, triumphing over them by the cross.' Or of the exalting cry of the elders round the throne in Revelation 5 who hail the victory of the slaughtered lamb: 'Then one of the elders said to me, "Do not weep! See, the Lion of the tribe of Judah, the Root of David, has triumphed. He is able to open the scroll and its seven seals"' (Rev. 5:5). We may think also of Jesus' description of his own task as the binding of the strong man so as to take possession of his goods (Mark 3:27). One of the central concerns of his ministry was undoubtedly driving out the forces of evil from ill and demented people – a theme that runs right through his ministry. All that is summed up in his claim in John to have overcome the world: 'I have told you these things, so that in me you may have peace. In this world you will have trouble. But take heart! *I have overcome the world'* (John 16:33).

Such passages make clear not only that this metaphor has sound scriptural roots, but also that its joyful celebration of God's ultimate victory, over all the dark powers that oppose him, does indeed proclaim that the battle Jesus fought is decisive for us all. From the cross Christ leads in triumph his conquered enemies; by the victory of the lamb the destiny of us all has been delivered into his hands, by what he did on the cross the world has been overcome.

(ii) Its Strengths

Furthermore one of the great advantages of this *Christus Victor* model is the way it integrates Christ's death with his resurrection. This is more than can be said of some of the theologies of the cross that have been prevalent, especially in the Churches of the West. Here cross and resurrection are seen as complementary, the cross the place of battle and Easter the resultant victory: the beginning of the new victorious life in which sin and death and hell have lost their destructive potential and are led, captives to his purposes and the servants of his will. And of course the uniqueness of the resurrection serves itself to highlight the decisiveness of the cross. There is something final and ultimate about a battle whose victorious protagonist rises from the dead.

(iii) Its Limitations

Nevertheless, this model, if not handled with caution, can easily lead us astray.[10] If the battle metaphor is not interpreted in the closest connection with the gospel narratives, it can, as its record in the history of theology shows, be developed in ways that are seriously one-sided and misleading, the chief of which are as follows.

Christ's triumph can be understood mythologically, in a way that severs it from the earthbound reality of what actually happened on Calvary and escapes into an intangible up in the air kind of world where great forces of divine and demonic power struggle for domination in a way more reminiscent of Captain

Kirk and *Star Wars* than of the gospel story. If the metaphor is cut
loose from the narrative, it can open the door to all sorts of
uncontrolled speculation about the powers of darkness and the
tactics by which they were and are to be defeated. Such specu-
lations abound in the writings of such unlikely bedfellows as
some of the Early Fathers and some of the more extreme demon-
ologists that in our day have sprung up on the lunatic fringe of
the charismatic renewal. All such speculation must be disciplined
by the reminder that the victory we are talking about – and the
only victory that matters – was the one that Jesus achieved on
the cross.

Closely connected is the warning that Christ's triumph is not to
be understood triumphalistically. This victory was won not by a
divine superman hurling supernatural laser beams of irresistible
energy against a cowering demonic host, but by a lonely suffering man in physical agony, forsaken by his friends and his
Father. A man suffering the worst that the forces of evil can do to
him, manifested as they are in the people who contrive his death
and the religious and political systems that have shaped these
people and that they are concerned to protect and defend. The
Lord is incarnate as he fights the battle, and so in their way are
the spiritual forces that attack him through Caiaphas and Pilate
and the rest.

Jesus wins not by exercising superior power but by submitting
to the worst that his enemies can do to him. His only power, and
by implication our only power as his people, is the power of the
love in which he identifies himself with the perpetrators who are
also the victims of evil and gives himself in interceding self-
offering to the Father on their behalf. The only power that is
stronger than the demonic evil that evinces itself personally and
structurally at every level of human life is the power of Calvary
love. That and no other is the decisive battle that is fought on
Good Friday and won on Easter day.

Again closely connected, we need to remember that on the
cross Jesus conquers evil not by a headlong confrontation with it
but by dealing with God from the midst of it. What we hear from
his lips on Calvary is not exorcistic battle cries addressed to his
enemies but interceding prayers addressed to his Father. When
he is being overwhelmed by evil, he deals with God. Here also his
way is to be ours. To defeat evil, we do not confront evil and
certainly do not become interested in it or fascinated by it; rather

we 'put on the whole armour of God' (Eph. 6:13). The best exorcism is intercession; the best defence against evil is a fresh self-giving in Christ to the Father. If that was always remembered, many disasters would be avoided, many victories won.

Such practical safeguards rest on the firm theological basis that on the cross Jesus is interacting chiefly with his Father. As Moltmann rightly says, the cross is an inter-Trinitarian event where everything turns on the Son's relationship to the Father and the resultant release of the Spirit. This is to some extent obscured by the battle metaphor where the interaction is between God, the Father and the Son on the one side, and his enemies on the other. This model, unlike some others, has the advantage of stressing the unity in purpose and action of Father and Son, but it does not allow for the personal differentiation between them which is central to the gospel narrative and is the presupposition of both the Son's intercession to the Father on the cross and his cry of dereliction from it.

All in all then, we may perhaps conclude that the *Christus Victor* theme is on the one hand undoubtedly a fruitful approach to the cross. Its dramatic simplicity and directness makes it effective in Christian preaching and hymnology and it affirms in no uncertain terms the decisiveness of the cross. On the other hand, despite Aulén's claims, it does not provide a framework for the comprehensive interpretation of Christ's work and can easily lead us off in directions whose theological inadequacy and practical dangers we have been trying to outline.

(b) The Sacrifice Metaphor

Our second atonement metaphor, that of sacrifice, is strong precisely where the battle metaphor is weak. Here the interaction between the crucified Jesus and his heavenly Father is at the very centre of the picture, although of course their identity is still affirmed, as we shall see. What is being described is, again in Trinitarian terms, a decisive self-offering to the Father by the Son on behalf of his people that removes the pollution of sin that stood between them and brings them into holy fellowship with each other once again.

(i) Its Credentials

The interpretation of Christ's death as a sacrifice is common to
nearly all the New Testament writers, but it is the Letter to the
Hebrews that develops it most fully as its central theme. From
one point of view the Hebrews theology of sacrifice is inaccessible to modern minds, because it is framed in contrast to the Old
Testament sacrificial system which is culturally alien to us and
whose rationale even the experts find hard to fathom. On the
other hand, one of the chief contrasts that Hebrews makes
between the Old Testament sacrificial system and the sacrifice of
Christ is that in the latter the differentiation between offering
priest and offered victim is abolished and replaced by the notion
of self-sacrifice, where the priest offers himself. This has the effect
of removing the whole notion of sacrifice from the context of
temple worship and making it entirely accessible and, indeed, the
primary meaning that the whole notion of sacrifice conveys. We
do not know about priests sacrificing animals on altars, but we do
know about people offering themselves, sometimes to the death
for the sake of others, and that gives us access to what Hebrews
most wants to say to us.

(ii) Its Strengths

It will be helpful to look one by one at some of the central
emphases that the sacrifice model helps us to keep in mind. Let
us begin with Hebrews 8:27–8: 'Unlike the other high priests, he
does not need to offer sacrifices day after day, first for his own
sins, and then for the sins of the people. He sacrificed for their
sins once for all when he offered himself. For the law appoints as
high priests men who are weak; but the oath, which came after
the law, appointed the Son, who has been made perfect for ever.'

The Identity of Priest and Victim

'He offered himself.' The identity of priest and victim gives this
sacrifice a moral and spiritual value that no temple sacrifice could
emulate. The victim is a willing victim; he does not, in Johannine
terms, have his life taken from him – he lays it down in the
service of the Father's purpose, which he has made his own. The
value of the sacrifice consists not in the *loss* of the life but in the
offering of the life in an act of free obedience. Hebrews has Christ
the High Priest address the God to whom he offers his sacrifice,

as follows: 'First he said, "Sacrifices and offerings, burnt offerings and sin offerings you did not desire, nor were you pleased with them" (although the law required them to be made). Then he said, "Here I am, I have come to do your will." He sets aside the first to establish the second' (Heb. 10:8–9). The offering is not the suffering as such or the death as such, but the ultimacy of obedience that will endure that suffering and death in willing affirmation of the Father's saving purpose. It is obedience that atones.

This differentiates Christ from all the unwilling victims of a dire fate that overcame them and over which they had no control. By his identification with them he takes them out of the realm of the oppression that has brought them where they are into the realm of the saving purpose that can move them towards liberation, because he who has come to them is, in his willing obedience, himself free.

A Sacrifice for Sin

'He sacrificed for their sins.' The aim of this sacrifice, as we have already seen, is the removal of sin. In order to achieve that, this priest acts in a representative and vicarious way, not on behalf of himself, but on behalf of others. This notion of vicarious representation is at the very heart of the being and function of a priest as it is at the heart of any sacrificial system. One man offers a sacrifice on behalf of many. Here this is affirmed of Christ in the sacrifice of his death, as it is affirmed right through the New Testament from the Last Supper narratives on. As we saw when we were discussing Fiddes, this notion of one person acting on behalf of another and doing for many people something that they could not do for themselves collides violently with the individualism of our culture and its demand for autonomy. We shall have to ask carefully how it is to be understood what Christ did and did not do for the rest of us.

A Single Sacrifice

'He sacrificed once for all when he offered himself.' The contrast he draws between the oft repeated, because ineffective, temple sacrifices, and the one unrepeatable sacrifice of Christ on the cross enables Hebrews to underline with great emphasis the *eph' hapax* – the once and for all character of the sacrifice of Christ – which is our own central concern.

What is offered once on earth has no need to be offered again either in earth or in heaven:

> For Christ did not enter a man-made sanctuary that was only a copy of the true one; he entered heaven itself, now to appear for us in God's presence. Nor did he enter heaven to offer himself again and again, the way the high priest enters the Most Holy Place every year with blood that is not his own. Then Christ would have had to suffer many times since the creation of the world. But now he has appeared once for all at the end of the ages to do away with sin by the sacrifice of himself. (Heb. 9:24–6)

This whole book could be understood as an exegesis of these verses; here we may simply note that in their light we need to be careful about the attribution to God of continuous involvement in all the suffering of his creation, as much modern theology has been wont to do in understandable reaction to the traditional doctrine of God's impassability. In Christ God suffered the consequences of sin once but does not suffer them in that way ever again. The Doctrine Commission of the Church of England spoke wisely when it said:

> Thus, just as the permanent availability of Christ our sacrifice needs expansion to be intelligible and defensible, so too does the parallel notion of a suffering God. For to make sense of the notion in both cases, we must surely speak of suffering that is of a different order and significance from that experienced on the cross: otherwise precisely the same objections that were once made to the agony of Christ being renewed in Catholic theology, must also now be raised against much Protestant theology.[11]

These two themes, the sense in which we can and cannot speak of a suffering God and 'the permanent availability of Christ our sacrifice' are both raised by Hebrews. The second poses us the question: How can a historical act done once affect those who are divided from it in time and space, how, in other words, can what is done once be for all? To answer that we shall have to draw out the implications of Christ's identity with his own sacrifice – 'He offered himself' – and of his eternal ascended presence at the right hand of God.

The Unique Person of the Priest

The uniqueness of the sacrifice is, for Hebrews, connected with the uniqueness of the person of the priest who offers it. The sacrifice renews the covenant between God and his people (8:7ff) and, to mediate its renewal, the priest must be identified with both parties. As we have already seen: 'He had to be made like his brothers in every way' (2:17), but equally he had to be identified with God. So in Hebrews: 'The Son is the radiance of God's glory and the exact representation of his being, sustaining all things by his powerful word. After he had provided purification for sins, he sat down at the right hand of the Majesty in heaven' (Heb. 1:3), and in 8:28 it is 'the Son who has been made perfect for ever' who is appointed high priest. The identity of the priest with God means that the sacrifice he offers is God's own sacrifice and has the permanent effectiveness and eternal validity that belong to the acts of God. It takes a high Christology to sustain a decisive sacrifice.

Sacrifice – A Great Simplicity

It has often been pointed out that Hebrews, like Leviticus before it, offers no rationale of sacrifice; they tell us what it achieves but not in any detail how it works. That may be because at the heart of it there is a great simplicity. In sacrifice through a representative offering, situations and people that have been closed to God are opened up to him. In a thank-offering, the good that has come is acknowledged to be the gift of God. In the fellowship offering, relationship with God is affirmed and renewed. In the sin offering, situations that have been closed to God by their rebellion and impurity are opened again to his cleansing and his changing. In the Passover sacrifice, the people – in remembering the decisive event of its history – opens itself up again in its present situation to the God who is the source of its life and freedom.

So in the sacrifice of Christ, from the midst of the suffering, desolation and death that encompasses him, Jesus offers himself to his Father in a submission, intercession and obedience that opens up that whole situation and the people who are involved in it to the forgiveness and new life that come from the Father. The distance between them and God is so great that only through his action can they have access to God and God to them. It is a situation that is dominated by destructiveness and death, so that only one who plunges into it and shares that death can open it up again to hope and to life. That is why, as Hebrews says: 'In fact, the law requires that nearly everything be cleansed with blood, and without the shedding of blood there is no forgiveness' (Heb. 9:22). Only where death is shared in the poured out life which is symbolised by blood, only there can the pardon of God penetrate and be effective.

We shall expand all these points as we proceed, but it is clear from what we have said already that the sacrifice metaphor as interpreted by Hebrews is still pregnant with significance for all who would understand the death of the Lord.

(c) The Reconciliation Metaphor

The third major metaphor of atonement is that of reconciliation, the restoration of good relationships between parties that have been at enmity with each other. Unlike the sacrifice model which at first sight looks alien and inaccessible, this metaphor makes an immediate and universal appeal. To be human means that the central factor of all our lives is the state of our relationships with other people on a personal level – within marriages and families, with employers, employees or colleagues in the world of work, between races and nations on the international scene – so that anyone who speaks in terms of the restoration of broken relationships will be sure of a hearing.

(i) Its Credentials

When Paul speaks in these terms, as he does in 2 Corinthians 5 and Romans 5, he is probably thinking in diplomatic rather than merely personal terms. For example he speaks in this context of our being 'Christ's ambassadors' (2 Cor. 5:20), the duly authorised messengers of a king who has made peace for his people and now calls on them to acknowledge that peace and make it their own. The reconciliation that Christ has effected is not a merely private and inward matter, it is a public reality that has its effects not just on a personal but on a cosmic scale; it is the reconciliation of the world (2 Cor. 5:19). If we, as we have done with the others,

ask what this model says to us about Christ's atoning work, the
following points need to be made.

(ii) Its Strengths

A Fulfilled Covenant

As we have already seen, our reconciliation with God is presented to us as a completed work, which we are indeed invited to
make our own, but in whose accomplishment we had no part:
'All this is from God, who reconciled us to himself through Christ and
gave us the ministry of reconciliation' (2 Cor 5:18). But we may
well ask how reconciliation, which inevitably involves two
parties, can be unilaterally brought about by one of them without
the co-operation of the other. If it takes two to make a quarrel,
then surely it also takes two to mend it.

To such a question the answer must be that Jesus is in such
identity with both the parties that he is able to act on their behalf.
In his identity with the Father he is able to act on the Father's
behalf in the initiative of his forgiving and saving grace. That is
why Paul can say 'God was in Christ reconciling the world to
himself.' The act of Jesus is the act of God.

But equally as the man who has penetrated to the depths of our
humanity and our plight on the cross, he is qualified to answer on
our behalf. From the midst of the human mess he speaks and
enacts our Yes to God. He is the man God has always been
looking for who shows himself to be God's man fulfilling the
covenant; the man who on the cross loves the Lord his God with
all his heart and soul and mind and strength and his neighbour,
and indeed his enemy, as himself. From the midst of the cross,
where we speak our No to God, he speaks his Yes as one of us on
behalf of all of us, and the whole situation is transformed. Here is
the new man, the man of God's providing, the man who is God's
own Son, who is in complete unity with God's will and purpose
and so is at peace with him. As T. F. Torrance puts it:

> We are to think of the whole life and activity of Jesus from
> the cradle to the grave as constituting the vicarious human
> response to himself which God has freely and uncon-
> ditionally provided for us ... Jesus Christ *is* our human
> response to God. Thus we appear before God and are
> accepted by him as those who are inseparably united to Jesus

Christ our great High Priest in his eternal self-presentation to the Father.[12]

The way the reconciliation metaphor is used by scripture both emphasises the decisiveness of Christ's work on the cross over against our response to it by underlining its representative character and making it urgent for us to ask what we mean by, in Torrance's phrase, 'the vicarious humanity of Christ'.

Reconciliation is More than Forgiveness

This model reminds us that the cross achieves reconciliation as well as forgiveness; it is not just about covering sin, it is about changing people. To forgive the sin without changing the sinner is a recipe for future disaster, as we all know to our shame when we have to come again and again to confess the same sins that God has graciously forgiven but whose power over us has not yet been broken. What however the cross promises is reconciliation; the forgiveness that deals with the past is only the first step on the road that leads to the emergence, first in Christ and ultimately in us, of a new humanity that is at one with God, a humanity that mirrors back to him the covenant love and the holy purity that he shows to us and is not constantly marred by further outbreaks of our forgiven but unchanged hearts. God's forgiveness is free, but its perfecting in the death of the old humanity and the birth of the new, that cost the cross.

(d) The Redemption Metaphor

The costliness of the cross and the liberation that it brings are the central emphases of the fourth atonement model, which speaks of our redemption from our slavery to sin by Christ's paying the price of our emancipation. A typical verse would be 1 Peter 1:18–19: 'For you know that it was not with perishable things such as silver or gold that you were redeemed from the empty way of life handed down to you from your forefathers, but with the precious blood of Christ, a lamb without blemish or defect.'

The designation of Christ as lamb in this context reminds us that this model has strong connections with the Passover – which celebrated the release of God's people from Egypt and from death through the blood of the lamb on their lintels – and with the Passover meal, in which lamb was eaten. This in turn connects us with the paschal setting of the Last Supper in which Jesus offers his flesh and blood as the means of the eschatological liberation that he is about to accomplish. Mark in fact has him speaking in terms of this model about giving his life as 'a ransom for many' (Mark 10:51).

This model echoes much that we have already learnt from the others. Its emphasis is prospective rather than retrospective; it points forward to future liberation rather than back to pardon for the past. In inviting us to see ourselves as slaves and captives of our own sinfulness who have to rely on the costly self-giving of a Liberator, it again underlines the decisiveness of Christ's vicarious action on our behalf.

We have one more atonement metaphor to look at; that of the law courts and the Judge who passes sentence in them. That has been the dominant model especially in the West and it requires a chapter to itself. As we turn to it we take with us all we have learnt of the crucified Lord who is victor in the battle, sacrifice on the altar, reconciler in the quarrel and liberator in our slavery and ask what it means that we should be judged in his court.

5

One Cross – Propitiation or Punishment?

To engage with what Aulén calls the Latin theory of the atonement is to enter a minefield that, if we are not very careful, will either explode in our faces or make us so careful and timid at every step we take that we shall never get through. For here is a maze of conflicting exegesis of biblical texts, semantic confusion where the same words are used with different meanings, and theological debate about, for example, whether this understanding of the way God's justice operates is itself just.

All this is often complicated by heavy emotional commitments on either side. On the one hand phrases like 'penal substitution' become slogans that define theological and ecclesiastical parties, so that to question them, even on biblical grounds, is seen as betrayal. On the other hand this whole approach can be summarily dismissed as outmoded and unacceptable in a culture that finds it difficult to relate to its leading concepts, with the result that what is being said, however valuable, can no longer be heard. Even in evangelical churches, where it has the status of official doctrine, it is often more formally affirmed than convincingly explained and preached.

It is good therefore, as we enter this dangerous territory, to remind ourselves of our main intention. It is not to deal with the whole complicated history of this strand of atonement theology, which has dominated the thinking of the Western Church for many centuries, but simply to learn what it has to teach us both positively and negatively about the significance of Christ's cross. Its source is undoubtedly the New Testament and, in particular, the letters of Paul and, for anyone with a biblical conscience, that is more than enough to gain it a sympathetic hearing and an attentive respect.

The Legal Metaphor

1. Its Credentials and its Strengths

With this model we supplement what we have learnt from the battlefield and its victories, the tabernacle and its sacrifices, the world of diplomacy and its peace treaties, the slave market and its costly liberation, by a visit to the law courts with their judges, their laws, their verdicts and their sentences. In the New Testament these models are not dealt with separately one by one, as we have been doing for the sake of clarity. Paul can move with ease from one to the other almost in the same sentence if such a combining of metaphors can help him to make clear the saving significance of the cross.

Our business now is to look at the Pauline teaching in which, always in rich combination with the others, the forensic model predominates and ask ourselves again, as we have done with them: what it is about the cross that this approach clarifies and emphasises? We can again do this point by point.

(a) The Reality of Judgement and Wrath

The forensic model underlines the reality of the wrath and the judgement of God as essential presuppositions for making sense of the cross. Paul is quite clear that sin is not just a problem for us, it is also and primarily, so to speak, a problem for God. He writes in Romans 8:1: 'Therefore, there is now no condemnation for those who are in Christ Jesus' which clearly implies that, apart from Christ Jesus, in God's court humanity stands condemned – and as Romans 6:23 makes clear, condemned on a capital charge, condemned to death. All Paul's language about justification by grace through faith in Christ, being acquitted of sin and entering into right relationship with God as a result of the cross, carries the same implication; apart from Christ there is no acceptance, the guilty verdict stands.

The same point is made in terms of the more personal reaction of wrath in Romans 1: 'The wrath of God is being revealed from heaven against all the godlessness and wickedness of men who suppress the truth by their wickedness' (Rom. 1:18). It is important to realise that the wrath of God in this context is not some unruly aspect of his character that sometimes gets the better of him and breaks out in fury against certain people at certain times. As the Church of England Doctrine Commission say:

> We should not of course think of God seething with temper and resentment, ready to 'zap' us with his thunderbolt in due course, should we not obey him. The intention of the image is to tell us that God is utterly opposed to selfishness, social injustice and ruthless exploitation of resources. It tells us of the seriousness with which God regards human sin, that, though psychology and sociology may help explain the conditions which lead to the act, they do not exonerate: human wickedness remains a reality which precludes enjoyment of the vision of perfect goodness which is God.[1]

In the New Testament the wrath of God is not in any kind of contradiction to the love of God. It is because God is love and because he is compassionately committed to that love and the justice that asserts and preserves it, that he is committed with an equal passion against all that hinders, denies and attacks that love. A God who could condone what contradicts his love would not be serious about it. His wrath is his passionate protest against the lovelessness and injustice of human society and the people who comprise it: it is his No to those who are disturbing the peace and order of his creation by their self-concern and their apathetic connivance with the destructive forces that victimise and oppress. Those who have burnt with righteous indignation on behalf of just causes and oppressed people should have no difficulty in understanding the wrath of God and the judgement of God as the shadow side of his commitment to his justice and his love.

How Wrath Operates

In Romans 1:18ff Paul not only emphasises the reality of God's wrath but describes the *method* of its operation. The key word here is, in Greek, the verb *paradidonai* meaning 'to give over, to hand over' and it occurs in this short passage no less than three times. We are told that those who refused to acknowledge and glorify him as God, although he had revealed himself to them in the works of his creation, were handed over 'to sinful desires' (1:24), to 'shameful lusts' (1.26), to 'a depraved mind' (1:28). In other words, God's wrath manifests itself not in dramatic and punitive interventions, but in allowing people to go on, at least for a while, in the godless way they have chosen. A way which promised liberation and fulfilment but in fact delivers disintegration, degradation and ultimately death to those who persist in it.

C. H. Dodd used to argue from this that the wrath of God in the New Testament is seen as an impersonal process rather than a personal reaction. That however is to create a false dichotomy; while it is true that the wrath operates in the sort of process we have been describing, it is equally true that this is a process that God allows and indeed wills. 'God gave them over' in the three verses we have quoted records a deliberate and personal divine decision to leave people and situations to the destructive consequences that they themselves have incurred, and that is his wrath. Paul Fiddes puts it well when he says:

> To say that judgement is not a penalty imposed from outside human life, but a natural consequence flowing from the sin itself, is not at all to espouse an impersonal view of the wrath of God. If God is passionately involved in the life of his creation, guiding it and sustaining it from within, then he is involved in the process of natural justice. He consents in an *active* and personal way to the structure of justice in the world, and so this consent can truly be called the 'wrath' of God against sin which spoils his work.[2]

(b) Sin Results in Death

Understood in this light, Paul's statement that the wages of sin is death ceases to be merely an eschatological threat at the end of life and the end of the world and becomes almost a sociological description of what begins to happen here and now when people begin to live life in ways that deny and contradict God's purposes for them. When people become alienated by sin from God and from one another, a destructive element enters into their relationship, which first threatens and finally disintegrates the enterprises and institutions that depend on these relationships. Marriages end in divorces, industrial disputes end in strikes that bring productive activity to a standstill, international rivalries end in wars with the incalculable havoc that they bring. In all these situations there are both responsible evil-doers and unde-

serving victims and a whole spectrum of people who are in some
degree both, but in all of them there is a potential and sometimes
an actuality of death on a small or a large scale.

When God in his wrath leaves his people to their sinning, then
indeed the wages of sin is death. If, in his mercy, final execution
of that death-sentence is delayed, nevertheless we live in a world
that shows itself to live on death row, unless something happens
to change the verdict and set us free. Or we may put the matter in
a less Western and forensic and more Eastern and ontological
way and say that when we cut ourselves off from God, we cut
ourselves off from the source of life and we begin to die. Like
cut flowers we may bloom for a while, but the root from which
we could draw fresh life is gone.

So the No of God, the wrath of God, the judgement of God is an
eschatological reality that already looms over our lives and the
world in which we live them. The forensic view of the atonement
is right to emphasise that it is against that dire background that
the work of the cross is to be set. By the cross of Jesus God enters
in a new way into the sinful situation to which he has handed us
over, and does what needs to be done to bring us back out of his
wrath into his love, out of his condemning judgement into
his accepting grace. If we accept the dire diagnosis, then we have
the most urgent motivation for looking into what God was about
when he gave us his only Son so that those who believe in him
should not perish but have eternal life (John 3:16).

2. Is Atonement by Propitiation?

In such a context, the next question is obvious. How does the
cross of Christ deal with the judgement and the wrath of God
from which he comes to deliver us? The traditional answer of the
Western Latin-type theologies of atonement with which we are
dealing has been in terms of propitiation and punishment, the
former term relating more to wrath and the latter more to judgement. By his death Jesus propitiates God's wrath and bears in our
place the punishment that is due to our sin, so that the demands
of God's justice are met, the wages of sin are paid on our behalf
by him. It is to a brief examination of these two statements that
we now turn.

The debate about propitiation is made the more difficult by

three linguistic factors that we do well to identify before we start. In the first place the word is now almost a technical term confined to this realm of theological discourse so that it has no commonly agreed meaning. Reflecting this, its dictionary definition is very wide. The *Shorter Oxford Dictionary* defines it as, 'an act of propitiating; appeasement; conciliation; atonement; expiation'. Its use in atonement theology reflects this wide range, so that one has to gather from the context what each writer means by it. Further, the term has become a buzzword for certain kinds of evangelical orthodoxy, so that its use certifies soundness and to be wary of it is a sure sign of heretical tendencies, an approach to the whole matter guaranteed to generate more heat than light.

Further to complicate the matter the Greek term *hilasterion*, which the *Authorised Version* translated as propitiation, occurs in only four New Testament texts[3] none of which make its precise meaning clear, so that it can be credibly translated as 'means of expiating sin' (*NEB*) or 'atoning sacrifice' (*NIV*). The term belongs to sacrificial language and detailed definitions are sometimes sought from Old Testament references, but these are seldom conclusive and often reflect all too clearly the theological commitments of those who champion them.

From all this it must now be clear that here we find ourselves in the midst of the minefield and must pick our steps one by one and with great care.

(i) Jesus does not Propitiate God

One step we may however take with some confidence since it would have pretty wide agreement. Whatever propitiation may mean, it does not mean that the result of Jesus' work on the cross was to change his Father's attitude towards the sinful world from wrath to love, from rejection to acceptance. The biblical witness is clear that God's prior love for the world is the source and not the consequence of Christ's atoning death. For the truth of this we need only recollect again John 3:16: 'God so loved that he gave . . .' or Romans 5:8 where precisely in the context of a discussion of God's wrath Paul speaks quite unambiguously of God's prior love: 'But God demonstrates his own love (*ten heautou agapen*) for us in this: While we were still sinners, Christ died for us.'

If the fact that 'the Father himself loves you' (John 16:27) is not continually underlined and emphasised, we shall be in danger, on a theological level, of making an illegitimate Trinitarian schism between the Father and the Son and, on the level of spirituality, of encouraging people to hide behind the coat tails of a loving Jesus to shield them from the anger of a vengeful God. That is blasphemy against the Father and devastating in its pastoral effects on people. It may however be a consequence of careless talk about propitiation that can make the Father seem unrelentingly hostile to us till his wrath is appeased at the cross. P. T. Forsyth sorts out the wheat from the chaff when he says:

> It would be a useful exercise to go through the Bible and see what proofs you can get of Christ's reconciling God . . .God can never be regarded as the object of some third party's intervention in reconciling. If it were so, what would happen? There would be no grace. It would be a bought thing, a procured thing, the work of a pardon-broker.[4]

(ii) Does God Propitiate Himself?

There are however those, who, from Calvin on, recognise and affirm the prior love of the Father but still want to make propitiation a central category in their theology of atonement. They are sensitive to the dangers we have just outlined and, to make clear that God is the subject as well as the object of the propitiating act, they advance the claim that on the cross God in Christ was propitiating himself. So C. B. Cranfield, in his commentary on Romans 3:25, makes the following very careful and nuanced statement:

> We take it that what Paul's statement that God purposed Christ as a propitiatory victim means is that God, because in His mercy He willed to forgive sinful men and, being truly merciful, willed to forgive them righteously, that is, without in any way condoning their sin, purposed to direct against his very own Self in the person of his Son the full weight of that righteous wrath which they deserved.[5]

John Stott writes in similar vein:

> It is God himself who in holy wrath needs to be propitiated,

God himself who in holy love undertook to do the propitiating, and God himself who in the person of his Son died for
the propitiation of our sins. Thus God took his own loving
initiative to appease his own righteous anger by bearing it in
his own self in his own Son when he took our place and died
for us.[6]

I have great sympathy with the general approach to atonement
theology of both these writers and, like them, I want to assert the
destructive reality of the wrath of God, which we have deservedly incurred and from which the work of Christ on the cross is
our only deliverance. My only question is whether the propitiation language that they use, which, in any case, may have
less biblical foundation than they claim, is the best way of describing the motivation and effect of the atonement. Let me make
two points:

What does it really mean to say 'God propitiated himself'? Can
the verb really have the same person for its subject and object and
still retain its meaning? What is the distinction between the one
who does the propitiating and the one who is propitiated? If it is
a Trinitarian distinction between the Father who is propitiated
and the Son who propitiates, then we are back in all the theological and pastoral difficulties that we encountered above, of
which both Cranfield and Stott are well aware and which the
latter expressly repudiates.

The last sentence of the Stott quotation above suggests rather
that what we have here is a juxtaposition of the two divine attributes of God's wrath and God's love, so that the God who is
loving sends his Son to propitiate the God who is wrathful, but
how these two contradictory attributes cohere in the same divine
nature is left undefined. He makes that explicit when he says: 'If
it is God's wrath that needed to be propitiated, it is God's love
that did the propitiating.'[7] He then goes on to quote with
approval Forsyth's statement that it was not God's character that
was changed from wrath to love but God's treatment of us
that was changed by the cross.

Nevertheless, unlike Forsyth, Stott affirms a readjustment of
attributes within God that makes his new relationship to us possible, but gives no account of how that readjustment of attributes
relates to the unchanging character of God. In this whole matter
we do well to listen to Forsyth himself when he says:

Christ has been represented as enabling God to forgive by
enabling him to adjust his two attributes of justice and mercy
within himself ... as though an attribute were something
loose within God which he could manipulate – as though the
attributes of God were not God himself, unchangeable God
in certain relations. The attributes of God are not things
within himself which he could handle and adjust. An attribute of God is God behaving, with all his unity, in a
particular way in a particular situation.[8]

On the face of it the statement about God's self-propitiation is not
very coherent or self-explanatory. It seems to suggest that the
atonement is concerned with a manipulation of conflicting
internal attributes of the divine nature in order to enable him to
forgive and accept us.

(iii) Who Must Change – God or Us?

Propitiation language, however refined and nuanced, suggests
that the change that needs to be made in order to make reconciliation possible is a change in God rather than a change in us. But
as we have already seen, we will search in vain for a New Testament text that suggests that God needs to be changed in order to
be reconciled to us.

On the contrary it is we who need to be changed in order to be
reconciled with God. In Christ he has reconciled the world to
himself, by identifying with us and taking on himself the dire
consequences of our sinning. He has taken down to death the old
humanity that had incurred God's wrath, and by his perfect self-
offering to the Father, created a new humanity that reflects back
to the Father his own holiness and love and therefore is reconciled to him. Throughout the whole process God remains self-
consistent. In him wrath and love are not conflicting attributes
that need to be reconciled internally. On the contrary it is his one
holy love that makes him both repudiate sinners in their sinning
and at the same time move savingly in Christ to change them and
reconcile them to himself.

Propitiation language has at its heart a very right concern to
take the wrath of God seriously and to emphasise that our sinful
rebellion is a serious and indeed potentially fatal disruption of
our relationship with him. What I have been suggesting is that

these concerns can be expressed much more appropriately in ways that do not suggest that God has to be changed in order to relate to us and accept us.

In the end I think G. B. Caird needs to be listened to when he says:

> One term, however, notwithstanding its use in the *AV*, must be discarded from the start. There was not in 1611, nor is there today, any justification for the use of 'propitiation' in this connection. 'Propitiate' is a transitive verb which requires a personal object, and which entails a change of attitude in the person propitiated. But in the New Testament atonement in all its forms has its origin in the unchanging purpose and love of God.[9]

It is good, before we move on, to remind ourselves that the above debate, which can seem very technical, not to say nit-picking, is part of the search for a theology of atonement that can be expressed in a preaching and pastoral care that offers people, not a hostile deity who needs to be appeased by the death of Jesus, but our Father who so loves us that when we are deservedly dying in our alienation from him seeks us in his Son to deliver us from our sins and open us up again to his life-giving grace. That would be the desire of all involved in this debate and the only question is whether and to what degree talk of propitiation serves that common end.

(iv) Propitiation and Expiation

John Stott follows C. H. Dodd in making a clear distinction between 'propitiation' and 'expiation' as an interpretation of Christ's saving work. As he puts it: 'The crucial question is whether the object of the atoning action is God or man. If the former, then the right word is "propitiation" (appeasing God); if the latter, the right word is "expiation" (dealing with sin and guilt).'[10] Stott himself wants to maintain both, but his main concern, as we have already seen, is to defend the primacy of propitiation over expiation.

If, as we have argued above, there are doubts about the usefulness of propitiation language, it is equally doubtful whether expiation language is an altogether satisfactory substitute and whether the contrast between dealing with God and dealing with man in atonement is a justifiable one. The problem is not 'sin and guilt' as impersonal realities, but rather sinful and guilty people. Expiation is again a term that derives from a sacrificial system that consists in the offering of one impersonal reality (the sacrifice) for another impersonal reality (the sin) and that is a less than appropriate way in which to speak of the cross, as if suffering and death somehow wiped out guilt and sin.

The whole thrust of the theology of Hebrews is, in the light of the death of Christ, to re-interpret the impersonal exchanges of Old Testament sacrifice for the personal relationships of Christ's obedient self-offering to his Father on behalf of his people. That is why personal terms like reconciliation are more appropriate than impersonal ones like expiation. They remind us that what we are talking about is what it takes to re-establish good relationship between a holy God and a sinful people.

Furthermore, we cannot say that on the cross Jesus is *either* dealing with God in his wrath *or* dealing with people in their sins. As we saw in the last chapter, Jesus deals with sinners not by confronting their sinfulness directly, but by identifying himself with them and offering himself to God on their behalf. He deals with sinners by dealing with his Father. Because he is God and man all his dealings with humanity are also and primarily dealings with his Father; expiation language, particularly when it is contrasted with propitiation language, can obscure that fact.

Our conclusion of this search for appropriate atonement language must therefore be that models like self-sacrifice and reconciliation are more appropriate than either propitiation or expiation to describe what was happening when Jesus died.

3. Is Atonement by Compensation and Retribution?

We move on now to the next major section of our examination of the Latin or legal model, by asking what it is about the passion of Jesus that propitiates God and expiates sin. In terms of this model, the answer will be that it is his offering to God in our stead which can reconcile us to him because it is an appropriate compensation for our sins.

In different forms of the theory that compensation is seen in different ways. For Anselm, against the background of medieval feudalism, the death of Christ gives God the satisfaction for the wound inflicted on his divine honour by our sin; for Calvin and the Protestant Reformers in general, the suffering and death of Christ are the punishment, the wages of sin, the retribution that has to be inflicted to maintain the divine justice.

Some proponents of this view think in terms of the criminal law and the retribution it requires of criminals, which for serious offences is death. Strictly speaking it is to this criminal sub-model that the term penal substitution is most properly applied. Others think more in terms of civil law and think in more commercial terms of the damages it awards against those who deprive others of their rights. So God needs to be compensated for the damage that sinners have done to him and the death of Jesus is the compensation paid by the Son of God on our behalf to the Father. As the hymn puts it: 'There was no other good enough to pay the price of sin,' which, in the terms we have been using, affirms that expiation is brought about by compensation.

What however is common to all forms of this model is what we might call the *recompense principle*. In order that sinners may be forgiven and restored to good relationships with him in a way that meets the demands of his justice, his honour has to be satisfied, sinners have to be punished, the wages of sin have to be paid. To provide that recompense was impossible for us and would at any rate have been our final undoing; therefore Christ in his death did for us what we could not and now do not have to do for ourselves. In what follows we shall discuss this view mainly in its penal form where it is expressed in terms of criminal law because that is the form in which this model is most frequently advocated and in which its merits and demerits most clearly appear.

Before we do it is important to note that those who use this model do not use it in any exclusive way, and can thus escape some of its limitations. Calvin for example often speaks of the death of Christ in terms of propitiation and punishment: 'This is our acquittal; the guilt which held us liable for punishment was transferred to the head of the Son of God.'[11] There could not be a more succinct statement of the central convictions of penal substitutionary views of the atonement. But the same Calvin also has much to say about Christ's obedience and the central part it plays in our being reconciled to God. Suffering and death can indeed be seen in terms of required retribution and can be

brought under the rubric of deserved punishment, but not obedience. In his emphasis upon it Calvin is clearly moving beyond the
parameters of penal substitution with its reference to compen-
sating for the past to something much more positive that opens
the door to the future.

(a) Penal Substitution – its Strengths

The penal substitution model of atonement is criticised in much
modern scholarship and is sometimes written off as unworthy of
rational consideration in an age where its basic presuppositions
about the seriousness of sin and the reality of the just judgement
of God against it are no longer taken seriously. But it is precisely
in its affirmation of these things and of our inability to deal with
them on our own that this model is at its strongest. The cross
itself is the demonstration of the crucifying hostility of fallen
humanity to the holy love of God that is incarnate in Jesus, of the
righteous and negative judgement upon us that our corporate
deicide at Calvary incurs, of the great gulf that this exposes
between us and our Creator, of the dreadful cost that our liberation from this sinful alienation involves, and of the saving
intervention of Jesus as the only one who can deliver us from that
dire situation. These are essential elements in any theology of
atonement that can claim to be faithful to the New Testament
witness and the proponents of penal substitution are among
those who have maintained them when many others within the
Church were ignoring or denying them.

(b) Penal Substitution – is it Biblical?

We have still however to ask whether the biblical witness sup-
ports this view of Christ as the one who bore the punishment for
sin in our place. Stephen Travis,[12] in an important article, dis-
cusses, with a scholarly New Testament expertise far beyond my
competence, the main Pauline texts[13] that are used as a foundation for the view that God's justice required retribution and
that that retribution he took on himself in his Son on the cross.
Travis's conclusions are that these texts can and often have been
understood as supporting penal substitution, but that they can
equally well be taken to support a rather different view:

Rather than saying that in his death Christ experienced retributive punishment on behalf of humanity, Paul says that he entered into and bore on our behalf the destructive consequences of sin. Standing where we stand, he bore the consequences of our alienation from God. In so doing he absorbed and exhausted them, so that they should not fall on us. It is both true and important to say that he 'was judged in our place' – that he experienced divine judgement on sin in the sense that he endured the God-ordained consequences of human sinfulness. But this is not the same as to say that he bore our punishment.[14]

In taking this line Travis is by no means a lone voice. John McIntyre comments: 'I have . . . to say that the biblical status of the idea of punishment is not immediately self-evident. For example, I cannot find New Testament statements which outrightly affirm that the death of Christ was a punishment visited upon Jesus rather than upon the mass of sinful mankind.'[15]

Karl Barth whose chapter on the atonement is headed 'The Judge Judged in our Place', which certainly places him squarely within the Latin model of atonement, nevertheless does not believe that the execution of that judgement requires vicarious retribution:

We must not make this [the concept of punishment] a main concept as in some of the older presentations of the doctrine of the atonement (especially those which follow Anselm of Canterbury), either in the sense that by his suffering our punishment we are spared from suffering it ourselves, or that in so doing he 'satisfied' or offered satisfaction to the wrath of God. The latter thought is quite foreign to the New Testament.[16]

It is therefore, on a New Testament basis, perfectly possible to hold that Christ endured God's judgement on sin without holding that he suffered God's punishment for sin.

(c) Not Recompense but Elimination

All of that calls into question the biblical and theological credentials of the recompense theory on which this whole model is often based. We may instead hold on good biblical grounds that what the justice of God was seeking and providing in the coming and dying of the Son was not retribution for sin but its elimination by being absorbed and overcome by the holy love of God that entered its realm and ended its reign in Jesus. Justice is done when that reign is ended and sin's power is broken. That happens when Jesus on the cross takes the whole situation of humanity, justly condemned to death as a consequence of its sinning, and transforms it by opening it up again to the God from whom it has been alienated.

In Romans 6 Paul speaks of how Christ died not so much *for* as *to* sin: 'The death he died, he died *to* sin once for all; but the life he lives, he lives to God' (Rom. 6:10). And he twice exhorts his readers to live as those who in their unity with Christ have done the same (6:2, 11). Christ in his self-offering on Calvary has entered the realm of judgement and death that we have brought on ourselves by our sinning. This is not that he might endure an equivalent punishment, but to extricate us from that judgement by bringing us first through the perfect obedience of his own humanity back into a right covenant relationship with God, so that he is indeed our God and we are indeed his people.

Karl Barth puts the point like this:

> The decisive thing is not that He has suffered what we ought to have suffered so that we do not have to suffer it, the destruction to which we have fallen victim by our guilt, and therefore the punishment which we deserve. That is true, of course. But it is true only as it derives from the decisive thing that in the suffering and death of Jesus Christ it has come to pass that in His own person He has made an end of us as sinners and therefore of sin itself by going to death as the one who took our place as sinners. In His person He has delivered up us sinners and sin itself to destruction. He has removed us sinners and sin, negated us, cancelled us out: ourselves, our sin and the accusation, condemnation and perdition which had overtaken us. This is what we cannot do and are not willing to do.[17]

(d) Restorative Justice

God's justice is concerned less with punishing wrong relationships than with restoring right ones. Like the heroes of the Book
of Judges, Jesus is concerned with freeing the land from the evil
forces that have infested it and setting our humanity free from the
personal and social twistedness that is corrupting and destroying
it. In so doing he acts not to placate his Father on our behalf, but
on his Father's behalf to set us free and show himself to be indeed
a just God and a Saviour (Isaiah 45:21) as he has promised. He
puts us right with God not because he is punished in our place
but because he is right and does right in the eyes of his Father;
most of all on the cross.

His justice is less punitive than restorative, he rejects sinners in
order to transform them into people who reflect his own holy
love in their relationships with him and with one another. It is
that drastic transformation, that dying to sin and living to God,
that Jesus is accomplishing for all humanity on the cross. As
Colin Gunton puts it: the concept of the justice of God that is
operating on the cross is

> transformational rather than punitive or distributive. That
> is to say, it accepts human responsibility and culpability for
> the breach of the universal order which results from rebellion
> against God, but holds that justice is done not by the impo-
> sition of equivalent suffering ... but by the process of
> transformation in which the reconciliation of persons enables
> the acknowledged evil of the past to become the basis for
> present and future good.[18]

We shall be exploring these ideas further in the next more con-
structive chapter. However, perhaps enough has been said to
show that it is possible to construct on a biblical basis and in a
way that maintains the biblical essentials, an approach to the
justice of God and what it achieves on the cross that is not dependent on the principle of recompense and punishment that
underlies penal views of atonement.

By its very nature the penal model is backward rather than
forward looking in its orientation. The bearing of the punishment
deals with the sins of the past, but taken by itself does not say
anything about how the person is brought into new and trans-

forming relationships that will produce a new quality of life in the future. This is particularly evident in Anselm's concentration on satisfaction from the past. It is less so in the Reformers, who supplemented the penal model with teaching about how restored right relationships with God opened up a process of sanctification by which the pardoned person was changed and renewed.

Nevertheless, within its own terms of reference, the penal model leaves us with pardoned criminals rather than people participating in the new creation. We need a more comprehensive model of atonement that is, as the Scottish theologian John McLeod Campbell puts it, both retrospective in dealing with the past and prospective in providing for the future: that shows how on the cross Christ not only made an end of the old humanity but gave birth to the new.

(e) Penal Substitution and Resurrection

To make the same point in another way, the penal model as such does not quite know what to make of the resurrection. It gives birth to a spirituality that on the Catholic side is symbolised by a crucifix and on the Protestant by a preaching that is dominated by a one-sided preoccupation with sin and condemnation and the suffering of Christ as the price of our deliverance from it. The resurrection is seen only as the sign of the Father's acceptance of the sacrifice, his affirmation of the sufficiency of what has been done to secure our pardon, and as a rather disconnected promise of life after death to those who belong to Christ.

But for the New Testament cross and resurrection belong together as part of the one paschal mystery and are far more closely integrated than this model is able to allow. That is the central message of Romans 6, summed up in verse 10: 'The death he died, he died to sin once for all; *but the life he lives, he lives to God.*' For Jesus and for us the whole point of the dying to sin is the new living to God that that makes possible. The resurrection is the aim and the end of the crucifixion, it is for the joy that is set before him that he endures the cross and despises the shame and reaches his destination at the right hand of the Father (Heb. 12:2). In turn the gift of the crucified Jesus to us is not simply that we should be pardoned sinners but that, through our baptism into his death, we should emerge into new life with him: 'We were therefore buried with him through baptism into death *in order that, just as Christ was raised from the dead through the glory of the Father, we too may live a new life'* (Rom. 6:4).

The point I am making is not that those who teach penal substitution would deny any of this, because they certainly would not, but the punishment model makes it hard for them to integrate it into their understanding of the cross and sometimes undergirds a sin-soaked piety in which the joyful spirituality of new life and resurrection plays an insufficient part.

(f) Is Penal Substitution Just?

It can be cogently argued that in the phrase penal substitution, the adjective and the noun do not go well together. If one understands the atonement by the analogy of the civil law, it is comprehensible that one person can pay the damages imposed on the other. If one stays with the criminal law, it is not at all clear how one person's punishment can be justly suffered by anybody except the person who has incurred that punishment by his breach of the law. The illustration, beloved of evangelical preachers of this tradition, of the judge who pronounces sentence on the criminal and then divests himself of his robe, comes down from his judgement seat and says 'I will bear this punishment in your place' is, in terms of justice, a quite scandalous story and any legal system that allowed such a thing to happen would be an unjust system. Whatever the love and compassion of the judge, if the issue is indeed one of punishment, then the one who has sinned, and nobody else, must pay.

P. T. Forsyth protests against the whole idea that the Father could punish the Son. 'That', he says, 'is an entirely unthinkable thing. How could God punish Him in whom He was always well pleased? The two things are a contradiction in terms.'[19] It may be that that judgement is too severe. The more sensitive proponents of penal substitution would reply that Jesus was both punished by the Father in his capacity as our substitute but in submitting to that punishment was still in the Father's full favour as the Son who was fulfilling the saving purposes of his love.

But the penal substitution theory appeals to justice and it must answer the question: How can it be just to punish a righteous man for the sins of many unrighteous people? Pannenberg quotes D. F. Strauss's summary of the position of the sixteenth and seventeenth century Socinians on this matter:

Neither   merit   nor   guilt   and   punishment ... is
transferable ... Ethically religious guilt and punishment are
not, however, something objective like gifts of money – with
which the Church's orthodox doctrine did not hesitate to
compare them – but something personal bound to the individual. A debt of money is held to be satisfied when paid,
whether by the debtor himself or by another. A moral debt,
however, is not paid at all, unless it is atoned for by the one
who has incurred it.[20]

If one were to affirm that statement in its totality, one would have
to abandon any thought of the substitutionary nature of Christ's
work on the cross and collapse into the worst kind of individualism in which each must look to his or herself, alone. At the same
time it is hard not to assent to the argumentation that guilt and
punishment are not transferable, like money and fines, but intrin-
sically by their own nature and morally by every rule of justice
are inseparably attached to the person whose sinful acts have
incurred them. If we are to maintain the representative nature of
Christ's work on the cross, we must define it in some way that
does not involve saying that he was punished in our stead.

What if Jesus was not punished instead of us but, in fact, came
to us in the place where we were already being justly punished
and so identified himself with us there that on our behalf he did
something that turned the place of rejection into the place of
acceptance and the place of death into the place of life? Is that
something that one person can justly do for another and that a
just God can do on behalf of his people?

P. T. Forsyth helps us to see what is at stake here when he
insists, on the one hand, that Christ's suffering and death were
penal in that it was an entering into and sharing of the just
consequences of our sinning, but, on the other hand, he himself
was not being punished because he had committed no sin:

The sacrifice of Christ, then, was penal, not in the sense that
God was so punishing Christ that there is left us only
religious enjoyment, but in this sense. There is a penalty and
curse for sin; and Christ consented to enter that region.
Christ entered voluntarily into the pain and horror which is
sin's penalty from God. Christ, by the deep intimacy of his
sympathy with men, entered deeply into the blight and

judgement which was entailed by man's sin, and which must be entailed by man's sin if God is a holy and therefore a judging God.[21]

To go into a prison you do not need to be a condemned criminal, you can go in love to where the prisoners are being punished to do what needs to be done to set them free. That is something the one can do for the many, and that is something that God in Christ did for us.

These are questions we must explore in the next chapter where we move from critical appraisal to more positive construction. We have been arguing here that the Latin model of atonement in its penal substitutionary form has less biblical support than is often claimed and is open, especially in its talk of propitiation and transferred punishment, to more theological objections than it has been able to answer.

That does not however mean that its usefulness has been exhausted. Many of the questions it raises are the questions that are at the heart of the matter and that all atonement theology has to face. It was the Johannine Jesus himself who interpreted his cross in terms, not indeed of punishment, but of judgement, when he said: "'Now is the time for judgement on this world; now the prince of this world will be driven out. But I, when I am lifted up from the earth, will draw all men to myself." He said this to show the kind of death he was going to die' (John 12:31–3). What that once and for all judgement was, how it defeats the prince of the world and how it draws everyone to the cross where it was executed is the agenda, not just of this book, but of all whose faith is in the crucified and risen Lord.

6

One Cross – The Birth of the New Humanity

In the rather technical discussions of the last chapter with all their talk of propitiation and punishment we may seem to have wandered well away from the historical event on Calvary from which we started. But in fact, not all that far! What happened on Calvary was the execution of a sentence that depended on a verdict that had been reached by Jewish and Roman legal processes that all the gospels describe. That legal process may indeed have defined the event for both Caiaphas and Pilate, although the latter, as he washes his hands, shows every sign of being uncomfortable with its outcome.

For Jesus however the legal perspective, though not absent, is never primary. As he approaches the cross his eyes are not on his human judges, before whom he remains for most of the time silent, but on his Father. It is from his Father that he seeks and receives in Gethsemane confirmation of his vocation to Calvary. He goes to the cross not as a criminal who is to receive punishment, but as a Son who, out of his deeply intimate love for *Abba*, overcomes his shrinking horror of what awaits him and offers himself in an act of costly, loving obedience to the Father's redemptive purpose which is also his own. 'Going a little farther, he fell to the ground and prayed that if possible the hour might pass from him. "*Abba*, Father," he said, "everything is possible for you. Take this cup from me. Yet not what I will, but what you will"' (Mark 14:35–6). It is that obedience that turns an execution into a sacrifice, a judicial act of a human court into a personal transaction between a Father and a Son on behalf of their lost but still loved and chosen people. To be lost is to be at the same time valuable and unavailable and the Son demonstrates their value to his Father by coming among them to make them available by opening up the whole alienated human situation and offering it to God.

1. *The Crisis of the Covenant*

In that context of his relationship with his Father and the opening up of the sinful human situation to his holy love, Jesus prays on the cross. It is true, as we saw at the end of the last chapter, that he sees his passion as the *krisis*, the decisive act of God's judgement on the world. However, the judge is not the remote condemning figure whose main concern is the strict enforcement of the law but the Father whose main concern is to put to rights for his people what by their fault has gone disastrously wrong. This is the just God who is also a Saviour and whose justice is executed by the Son who cries for pardon for his crucifiers and who says to the hopeless criminal who turns to him: 'Today you will be with me in Paradise.'

To put the same thing another way, the Judge who acts at Calvary is not the Roman judge who acts according to Roman law, *lex*, balancing crime with punishment, injury with recompense. This is the Judge of the Old Testament law, the *Torah*, whose concern is to maintain and restore his covenant relationship with his people.

At the heart of that covenant is God's commitment: 'I shall be your God and you shall be my people',[1] which is a promise as much as it is a command. This covenant involved two parties but was made by one of them. It was God alone who determined that he should be Israel's God and that Israel should be his people; so it is God alone who can restore the covenant when it is broken. That is what he does in Jesus. In Christ on Calvary we see the depth of God's commitment to a people who have proved themselves entirely unworthy of it; this is how he will show himself to be our God.

At the same time God in Christ becomes the one true representative of Israel who keeps the covenant when all others have broken it. In the obedience of the cross the covenant is fulfilled from the human side when the Messiah of Israel offers himself to the God of Israel on behalf of the people of Israel. Here in the life and, climactically, in the death of Jesus, God not only finds, but himself in his Son provides, the man who keeps the covenant. In the dire and deadly situation where it seems to be finally broken when Israel crucified its God, the new people of Israel who love the Lord their God with all their heart and soul and mind and

well if this not wrong I don't know what is

strength and their neighbours, including their enemies, as themselves – that people is born.

Thus the cross is the *krisis*, the crisis of the whole history of
Israel, the judgement of God on the whole life of his people in the
most positive sense. Here he does for them what they could not
do for themselves: he rescues them from the deadly alienation
into which they have fallen, puts what is wrong to rights, fulfils
his covenant and in his Son makes his people acceptable to
himself. He can do this because in Jesus he finds his own holy
love mirrored and reflected back to him from the very midst of
the evil darkness of the cross.

Of course in all this we speak of Israel not exclusively but
inclusively. God's election of Israel is the preliminary step he
takes towards the election of all humanity. Israel's rejection of
God is the demonstration in one people of the alienation from
God of all people. The bad news is that what Israel did to God is
what we all have it in us to do to God; it provides no excuse for
any kind of anti-Semitism. The good news is that God's grace
towards Israel in the life and death of the Messiah is the grace that
comes from Israel to all the world. The promise to Abraham
that in his seed all the families of the earth would be blessed is
fulfilled in Jesus where the election of one people becomes the
election of all people, where the *krisis*, the saving judgement on
Israel, becomes the saving judgement on all the world. Jesus is
not just the ultimate Abraham, but the ultimate Adam. His
saving grace comes from one place, one time, one people, but it
bursts out to all places, all times, all people: "'Now is the time for
judgement on this *world*; now the prince of this *world* will be
driven out. But I, when I am lifted up from the earth, *will draw all
men to myself.*' He said this to show the kind of death he was
going to die' (John 12:30–3). It is once in Israel, but it is always for
all.

New Covenant – Relational not Legal

Thus the fundamental categories in which we are to approach the
event of Calvary are not the impersonalities of a legal system, but
the personal realities of the intimate relationship of the Father
and the Son interacting to restore right relationships with his
alienated people. To recover what he called a filial rather than a

merely legal perspective of the cross was one of the great achieve-
ments of that prince of atonement theologians, the Scotsman,
John McLeod Campbell, in his classic work, *The Nature of the
Atonement*. He says:

> Let us think of Christ as the Son who reveals the Father, that
> we may know the Father's heart against which we have
> sinned, that we may see how sin, in making us godless, has
> made us as orphans, and understand that the grace of God,
> which is at once the remission of past sin, and the gift of
> eternal life, restores to our orphan spirits their Father and to
> the Father of spirits His lost children.[2]

So, we are to speak of the cross in what McLeod Campbell calls
filial as opposed to legal terms. The aim and end of the whole
event is that we should in Christ and by the Spirit be so related to
God that we can come with confidence to *Abba*, Father, and know
ourselves to be his loved and accepted children.[3]

The Double Identification

If we go on to ask how this result is achieved, the answer is by a
double identification that leads to a total self-offering. Jesus is
able to bring our humanity back into reconciled relationship with
the Father because he is totally identified with both parties, eternally one with the Father and making himself in his incarnation
totally one with us. If it is God who made the covenant, it is God
who must renew the covenant; if it is by us that it was broken, it is
from our side that it must be restored. This is the point at which
we can see how Christology and Soteriology depend upon each
other. In his person he must be totally identified with God and
totally identified with humanity if in his atoning work he is to be
qualified to bring the two together again. We go on now to see
how that double identification is the context in which he effects
on the cross the decisive deed of our reconciliation. In this
chapter we shall concentrate upon his identification with us, and
in the next his identification with God, remembering throughout
that the two are so intimately conjoined that we cannot speak of
one without assuming the other.

2. *Christ's Identification with Humanity*

(a) In the Biblical Witness

The theme of identification runs through the ministry of Jesus
from start to finish, it holds together what he began at Christmas,
enacted sacramentally in his Jordan baptism, lived out in Galilee
and finally brought to its climax on the cross. By his birth of Mary
he is in Matthew's nativity story hailed as Immanuel, the God
who is with us as one of us. In the grand Johannine manner he is
the Word who has become flesh and dwelt among us; in the
baptism narratives he takes his place among the repentant
sinners who respond to John's message. Even though in his own
person he has nothing to repent, he stands with those who have
much to repent and takes up their cause.

That with which he identifies is flesh, not humanity in its
strength and innocence, but humanity in its weakness, its vulnerability, its blindness, its poverty, its ambiguity, its rejectedness. He
is as vulnerable as we are to temptation, 'tempted in every way,
just as we are' (Heb. 4:15), which means that that there was that in
him, just as there is that in us, which responds to and is drawn
towards the enticements that evil sets before us. Someone in
whose nature evil has no foothold is incapable of being tempted.
As Karl Barth puts it:

> He was a man as we are. His condition was no different from
> ours. He took our flesh, the nature of man as he comes
> from the fall. In this nature He is exposed every moment to
> the temptation to a renewal of sin – the temptation of
> impenitent being and thinking and speaking and action. His
> sinlessness was not therefore His condition. It was the act of
> His being in which He defeated temptation in His condition
> which is ours, in the flesh.[4]

Jesus' struggle with the demonic attack on his newly bestowed
messianic vocation in the wilderness was a real struggle that
took forty days of prayer, fasting and searching the scriptures to
resolve. He faced temptation on the same terms that we do; only
so has his victory over it – 'yet without sin' – any relevance to us.

Throughout his ministry he gave himself in healing and deliverance to those who were the victims of evil and identified

himself as the friend and liberator of all whom those who claimed to be righteous had cast out. It is therefore entirely consistent with this that he should in his passion bring this identification to its terminal climax, should declare himself on the night before he died to be giving his body and his blood 'for the forgiveness of sins', should in his death be numbered with the transgressors, should hang in the place where the wages of sin are visibly paid and should there offer himself in intercession for those who had sinned by putting him there.

That self-giving identification with the victims and even more with the perpetrators of evil is obviously of great importance for Paul. In Romans 8:2–3 the only way in which God can 'set me free from the law of sin and death' is by 'sending his own Son in the likeness of sinful flesh (*en homoiomati sarkos hamartias*) to be an offering for sin.' The word *homoioma*, here translated 'likeness', indicates on the one hand how deeply and fully Christ penetrated into the sphere of sinful flesh and yet at the same time how he held back from a total identification with sinful flesh. He wrestled with it without yielding to it; he stood with the sinners but he did not himself sin.[5]

Paul walks the same tightrope in 2 Corinthians 5:19, a verse that, were it not in the canon of Scripture and its author an apostle, would certainly be denounced as heretical by many proponents of so-called orthodoxy. 'God made him who had no sin to be sin for us, so that in him we might become the righteousness of God' (2 Cor. 5:21). We could well understand why the great New Testament scholar, Bengel, should have exclaimed of this verse: 'Who would dare to speak thus, unless Paul had led the way?' But Paul has led the way because the only Christ who could help us is the one who came and found us where we are and entered into the heart of our dire situation so that he might do something about it on our behalf. As C. K. Barrett puts it: '[Paul] says that Christ became *sin*; that is, he came to stand in that relation to God which normally is the result of sin, estranged from God and the object of his wrath.'[6] But of course it is equally important immediately to add that he who stood there was 'the one who had no sin', who, in his identification with us in our situation, was totally different from us in his own relationship with God. When he stood in what is, apart from him, the place of estrangement and wrath, he transformed it into the place of obedience and acceptance so that we could 'become the

righteousness of God in him' and so could enter into that right
relationship with God which he established by what he brought
to us and did for us in that place.

The identification of which we speak here is not assimilation: a
Christ who became in every respect the same as we are would be
as helpless as we are. The only reason for his identification with
us is that he should bring right into the heart of our situation
where he joins himself to us 'in the likeness of sinful flesh'; something that he has and we do not have, that is able to help us
because it does not belong to the sinful flesh.

Christ comes to the cross as the fireman comes to the fire, as the
lifeboat comes to the sinking ship, as the rescue team comes to
the wounded man in the alpine snow. They have what it takes
to help and deliver, but they must come to where the fire burns,
the storm rages, the avalanche entombs and make themselves
vulnerable to the danger that such a coming involves. So Christ
on the cross comes to where the Father in his holy wrath has
handed over the sinners to the consequences of their sin. As he
identifies with us in that situation, he brings to us and for us the
holy love that is his by nature but that he has worked into his
own humanity and in his ministry shown to us. As one of us,
standing where we stand, he offers himself to his Father on our
behalf in a holy love that is both divine and human, both the gift
of God to us and an offering to God in his shared humanity, made
on behalf of all humanity from the very depths of our sin. That is
the saving identification of him who is without sin but is made
sin for us.

(b) Deliverance is by Identification

It is only from the inside, by such an identification as we have
been describing, that evil can be overthrown. People sometimes
ask why the restoration of right relationships with God should
require the whole gruesome apparatus of Christ's crucifixion. If
there is in God the readiness to forgive and if there is in the
people who have sinned the readiness to repent, what more is
needed to bring the relationship between them back into good
order?

If we are talking only of forgiveness for past sins, the argument
has a certain plausibility, although Paul Fiddes has argued con-

vincingly that a genuine forgiveness requires in one who offers it the kind of costly absorption of the evil done that the New Testament affirms of Jesus on the cross. Before sin can be genuinely forgiven it has to be borne, for only by being borne can it be overcome. The one who forgives must come to:

> ... the point of thinking himself into the mind of the offender, feeling with the guilty person, standing in his shoes and making a deep effort to understand why he said or did what he did. Only when the forgiver has made this costly journey of sympathy into the experience of the other can he go to him and say 'I forgive you'.[7]

That may indeed indicate part of what is happening when Jesus enters into the sinful situation to bring forgiveness to sinners.

But God's purpose in Christ is not simply to forgive, in the sense of not holding the past against his people any longer. His purpose, which, as we have seen, has its sole origin in his own prior love for us, is not simply pardon, but reconciliation, the bringing of two parties together in a relationship where harmony of mind, purpose and nature is restored and maintained between them. To forgive and to leave the forgiven party unchanged is simply to invite the disharmony of the past to break out again in the future. As Geoffrey Paul puts it:

> ...when sin has really got its grip on a situation, offers of forgiveness and individual attempts to do better are in the end insufficient, ineffective and marginal in their effects. Some sort of death is the only way in which the canker in the whole system can be attacked and overcome. Repentance and forgiveness do not deliver the penitent *from the situation*, do not strike at the root of his predicament. Only a total remedy affecting the situation as a whole can offer the individual any real hope of a new start.[8]

It takes something more radical than pardon to deal with the hold of evil within us and around us. The purpose of God in Christ is not simply, in the words of the Lord's Prayer, to forgive us our trespasses; it is also to deliver us from evil. Evil cannot be dealt with either by force or by fiat. The force of Peter's sword on the natural level and the twelve legions of angels on the supernatural level are alike powerless to achieve what could only be achieved on Calvary. If the house of the strong man is to be possessed, the strong man must first be bound (Mark 3:27) and the champion who would bind him must come to close grips with him, with all the exposure and danger that involves. If Jesus does indeed cast out the demons with a word, it is not the word of disengaged omnipotence but the word of the incarnate Son who has come into the sphere where the demons exercise their power and is on his way to his final confrontation with them on the cross.

Law and the enforcement of law can at best restrain and control evil for a time, and that may often be the only appropriate response in the short term. However Jesus on his way to Calvary is concerned not with proximate but with ultimate solutions and the inner logic of the cross is that evil can be overcome only by being borne. If the only thing that is stronger than evil is God's holy, creative and renewing love, then that love must come where evil victimises people with its hate and destructiveness. We cannot be liberated by a love that stays secure in heaven but only by a love that hangs on a cross. The victims of suffering can be released only by a love that suffers with them and brings into the situation a new factor that will liberate them from it. Sinners can be set free from the deadly consequences of their sinning only by one who shares these consequences with them so that love encounters hate on its own ground and makes peace in the midst of violence and does right amidst wrong. A way through death can be made only by one who has died, ultimate destruction can be overcome by ultimate love only through one who has himself been totally destroyed. The raising of Lazarus by a still-living Jesus is only a preliminary cheating of death; the sting of death is finally drawn only when Jesus himself has died and risen again.

That evil is conquered only when it is borne in the hidden wisdom of God of which Paul speaks in 1 Corinthians and which is hidden from both Greeks and Jews:

> Jews demand miraculous signs and Greeks look for wisdom, but we preach Christ crucified: a stumbling-block to Jews and foolishness to Gentiles, but to those whom God has called, both Jews and Greeks, Christ the power of God and the wisdom of God. For the foolishness of God is wiser than man's wisdom, and the weakness of God is stronger than man's strength. (1 Cor. 1:22–5)

If we take our bearings from Christ crucified we quickly become aware of the ultimate impotence of mere omnipotence and the ultimate sovereignty of the weakness of the man hanging in love on his cross. When people ask why God does not do something about some evil situation, the Christian answer must be that he has done the only thing that is ultimately relevant to its overcoming: come into it in his love on Christ's cross.

(c) By Identification Humanity is Transformed

The victory of the love of God in Christ is won in our humanity and it results in the transformation of our humanity so that it is no longer in alienation from God. Instead it has become responsive and open to him and, as was intended from its creation, the mirror in which his image is reflected. His incarnation is the primary expression of his love that makes all the other expressions possible. It is because he is one of us that he can teach us in a human language, call us into a human fellowship, heal us with a human hand, and enter with a human body and blood into our sufferings and the alienation from God that causes them.

In so coming into our humanity he changes and transforms it, first in himself vicariously on our behalf and then through his Spirit personally and corporately in us. What he does with the humanity he takes is both negative and positive. Supremely through his cross the old humanity of the sinful flesh is taken down to death. The No that God speaks against it is executed and exhausted and on the same cross the new humanity to which the Father speaks his just and accepting Yes is brought to birth. The negative is for the sake of the positive; the death of the old is for the sake of the birth of the new. The retrospective condemning judgement on the past is for the sake of the prospective accepting judgement of the future. It is to emphasise that positive thrust of Christ's atoning act that we have called this chapter the birth of the new humanity.

The Johannine Christ himself makes use of the notion of the eschatological birth pangs of the coming new age when he is speaking to his disciples about his approaching death: 'A woman giving birth to a child has pain because her time has come; but when her baby is born she forgets the anguish because of her joy that a child is born into the world' (John 16:21). In his day more

than in ours, the birth of a child was a hazardous business and
the pain and labour of it was itself seen as one of the consequences of sin (cf. Gen. 3:16) but the bearing of the pain was for
the sake of the joy that a new life has been brought into the world.

Still in John, Jesus in his crown of thorns and already on his
way to the cross is prophetically hailed by Pilate as *ho anthropos*,
the real man, the prototype of humanity as it was made and
meant to be (19:5). The Pauline Adam typology in Romans 5
and 1 Corinthians 15 points in the same direction. Jesus as the
eschatos Adam is contrasted with the *protos* Adam; the latter is a
living being, the latter life-giving spirit (1 Cor. 15:45). In solidarity
with the first Adam we are in the control of sin and bound for
death, but in solidarity with Christ we are brought into right
relationship with God and are bound for life.

It is true of course that the *eschatos* Adam is the risen Christ
who gives us his Spirit, the life of the new man is a risen life, but
that risen life is a consequence of the birth of the new man amidst
the death of the old, and that happens on the cross. The 'therefore' of Philippians 2:9 is pivotal at this point. It looks forward to
the exalted life which the risen and ascended Lord lives at the
right hand of the Father: 'Therefore God also highly exalted him
and gave him the name that is above every name, so that at the
name of Jesus every knee should bend' (Phil. 2:9–10). But it also
looks back to the one who did not, like Adam, count equality
with God something to be grasped but modelled a new humanity
in the humility and self-emptying of his life. A life which came to
a culmination in his obedience in the place that was furthest
away from the glory from which he had started: 'He humbled
himself and became obedient to the point of death – *even death on
a cross. Therefore . . .*' (Phil. 2:8–9). This is indeed a new kind of
humanity whose cradle is a cross.

The same theme is carried further in the Letter to the Hebrews
where, as we have already seen, the human solidarity and
empathy of the High Priest who acts atoningly on our behalf is at
the very heart of the message: 'For the one who sanctifies and
those who are sanctified are of the same family. For this reason
Jesus is not ashamed to call them brothers and sisters' (Heb. 2:11).
But what the High Priest does on our behalf is to offer a human
obedience and it is that human obedience in which our wills
correspond to God's will that is the essence of the new humanity.

(d) Vicarious Obedience Atones

It is in terms of that obedience that the cultic notion of sacrifice is redefined. 'First he said: "Sacrifices and offerings, burnt offerings and sin offerings you did not desire, nor were you pleased with them" (although the law required them to be made). Then he said, "Here I am, I have come to do your will." He sets aside the first to establish the second. And by that will, we have been made holy through the sacrifice of the body of Jesus Christ once for all' (Heb. 10:8–10).

Sacrifice is re-defined as obedient self-offering, not therefore simply the obedience of particular acts but the obedience expressed in the self-giving of the whole person. Furthermore that obedience comes to its perfection in the suffering of the cross and it is only as the ultimate and costly expression of that obedience that his suffering has value with God. As Forsyth puts it: 'The atoning thing is not obedient suffering but suffering obedience. He could be satisfied and rejoiced only by the hallowing of his name, by perfect and obedient answer to his holy heart from and amid conditions of pain, death and judgement.'[9] In the same way, to return to Hebrews, that obedience effects our eternal salvation by eliciting a corresponding obedience in us: 'Although he was a son, he learned obedience from what he suffered and, once made perfect, he became the source of eternal salvation for all who obey him' (Heb. 5:8–9).

Thus in the midst of the desolation and judgement of Calvary the new obedient man, the first fruits and the promise of a new kind of humanity that at last obeys God's commandment, reflects back God's holiness and fulfils God's covenant from the human side. The suffering of Jesus in the place of abandonment, where God seems to be absent, is not simply the consequence of other people's sins but becomes in him the enactment of that trustful surrender to the Father's will with which he emerged from the agonising wrestling of Gethsemane: '*Abba*, Father, not my will but yours be done.' Where that is not only said but done from the midst of the human mess the new man is born.

All this can be said equally well in terms of the legal model of atonement. This new man, because he has perfectly fulfilled the covenant and been totally obedient to the Father's purpose, is now himself in right relationship with the Father so that the requirements of the divine justice are fulfilled and the Father's verdict on what he has done in his identification with us can be expressed in his being raised from the dead. The verdict of the unjust courts of Israel and Rome is quashed by the verdict of the supreme court when the Judge of all the earth decrees that this new man shall not die but rise and live at his right hand.

(e) Identification Achieves Reconciliation

The decisive atoning act of this new man is to open the fatally alienated human situation, with which he has identified himself, up to God as by his vicarious obedience he brings it back into a right covenant relationship to his Father. Because this new man is in right relationship to God and because he has identified himself with the sinful human situation, he is able to open the one up to the other so that the abandonment of wrath that sin and sinners had justly incurred is replaced by the acceptance of grace and the transforming and life imparting gift of the Holy Spirit who is breathed out on the disciples as a result of the finished work of Christ on the cross. The handing over to sin is replaced by the handing over of the Holy Spirit, as the use of the very same Greek word in John 19 makes clear. The dying Jesus who has just cried in triumph *Tetelestai*, it is completed, 'bowed his head and handed over his Spirit *(paredoke to pneuma)'* (John 19:30).

The re-establishment of positive relationships between God and humanity which results in a new dynamic flow of life from the one to the other is the common factor at the very heart of all the New Testament models and metaphors of atonement. In Paul's use of the legal metaphor the purpose of the justification of sinners is not the restoration of a righteous order as such, but the re-establishment of the dynamic flow of life from God to us. So in his comparison of Adam and Christ in Romans Paul looks to the ultimate result of what the latter has done: 'Consequently, just as the result of one trespass was condemnation for all men, *so also the result of one act of righteousness was justification that brings life for all men'* (Rom. 5:18).

In our culture talk of obedience is often seen to imply the oppressive claim of a superior upon an inferior, but the obedience of Jesus to his Father cannot be understood in these terms. It has value only as his free act undertaken in personal trust of his Father, but just because it is obedience to the Father who is the source of freedom and life, it is an obedience that brings freedom and life to him and through him to us. The road he walks in his obedience is the road to resurrection. His kind of obedience is the key, not to clang the door of the prison shut, but rather to throw it wide open.

We have already seen how in Hebrews the result of Christ's obedient self-offering is the creation in us of an obedience like his that brings us into a new life like his. In the closest connection with the reconciliation motif in 2 Corinthians Paul speaks of a new creation: 'Therefore, if anyone is in Christ, he is a new creation; the old has gone, the new has come! All this is from God, who reconciled us to himself through Christ and gave us the ministry of reconciliation' (2 Cor. 5:17–18). The new humanity that was born on the cross is imparted to us as we enter into the reconciliation that Christ has effected at the cross.

In that stream of modern atonement theology that starts with McLeod Campbell and flows through Moberly to Forsyth, the emphasis on the positive and forward looking aspects of the work of Christ is maintained and the way they describe it reflects that fact. This is not the place to expound that theology in detail but the way that it speaks of Christ's atoning work in terms of intercession, vicarious repentance and the confession of God's holiness serves to underline its purpose as the re-opening of our alienated humanity to the source of its life and freedom in God.

(i) Obedient Intercession for Us

To see Christ's cross as an act of *intercession* is of course to make renewed contact with the passion narratives themselves, especially that of Luke which is introduced and defined by the prayer, 'Father, forgive them, because they do not know what they are doing.' This intercession is not to be understood as the pleading of a loving Son with an implacable Father for a pardon that he is reluctant to offer, but rather as the opening up of the whole abandoned human situation to God by bringing it out of its abandonment back into relationship with him. The new humanity is an interceding and praying humanity and that is both pleasing to God and profitable for the rest of us who in our ignorance of what we are doing cannot pray for ourselves. As McLeod Campbell himself puts it:

With all the weight of all our need upon His spirit – bearing our burden – that He should cast this burden upon the Father appeared the perfection of sonship towards the Father and brotherhood towards us. And as this intercession seemed a natural form for the love of Christ to take, so did it seem what must be to the Father a sacrifice of a sweet-smelling savour; and we felt that no aspect of the perfect sonship in humanity which the life of Christ presented to the Father could be more welcome to the heart of the Father than that of love to men, His brethren, as thus perfected in intercession; especially as being intercession for brethren who also were enemies, making the intercession to be the perfecting of forgiving love.[10]

(ii) Obedient Repentance for Us

But if the new humanity is an interceding humanity it is also a repentant humanity. This was the particular emphasis of R. C. Moberly in his classic work *Atonement and Personality*, where he explains what he means by repentance or penitence in this way: 'For this is penitence; perfect re-establishment of the absolute personal identity with righteousness, in the form of unreserved embrace of whatever is necessary to consummate the perfect condemnation of sin.'[11]

We need to pay careful heed to that definition if we are going to speak of repentance in connection with Christ's work on the cross, noting both what it excludes and what it asserts. It excludes the notion of compensatory repentance, which has been at the heart of the penitential system of the Latin West. We have already rejected the idea that Christ is punished to make up to God for sin, and we are therefore equally bound to reject the idea that the cross is an act of compensatory penitence for the sins of the world.

Equally we cannot understand Christ's repentance as involving a personal repudiation of personal sin. The one thing he cannot say is, 'I am sorry for what I have done'. A third party, however identified with sinful men and women in the shame and alienation that their sins incur, cannot confess other people's sins. Inasmuch as repentance involves saying, 'I did it', Jesus cannot repent on our behalf. That is something we have to do *for* ourselves even if we cannot do it in any complete way *by* ourselves.

The repentance in humanity that Jesus brings about in his life and his death is not *poenitentia* but *metanoia*. Not sorrow and contrition for personal sinning, but a change of mind and attitude in our humanity that from the midst of a situation dominated by rebellion against God turns it all round by making that same situation the locus for the supreme act of obedience to God. The act of Jesus is that turning round, that conversion of a human nature – in Luther's phrase, *inurvatum in se* – turned in on itself and so resistant and recalcitrant in its relations to God and to others that it becomes a renewed human nature that is turned outwards in its free and unconditional self-giving to God and to others. That is the change of mind and heart that Jesus accomplishes for our humanity when amidst the deluded self-assertion and self-preservation that bring about his crucifixion, he offers himself to his Father on behalf of his enemies. That is his repentance.

That kind of repentance (*metanoia*) is possible only because he has no need for the other kind of repentance (*poenitentia*) because he has no sin of his own to confess. The only one who can effect repentance for others is he who has nothing for which to repent. The only one who knows the awfulness of sin in the light of the holiness of God and what needs to be done to purge it is the one who himself perfectly mirrors that holiness and is therefore qualified to deal with the whole situation in a way that corresponds to his Father's purpose and will. Jesus has that 'perfect identity with righteousness', of which Moberly speaks, that alone can make an end of sin. Just as a doctor cannot provide a reliable diagnosis, let alone a cure for his own illness, so all of us who are far distant from God in our alienation from him, who, in Paul's phrase, have a mind that is 'hostile to God' (Rom. 8:7), are in no position to fathom the depths of what is wrong with us, still less to know what needs to be done to put it right.

So we are left with the paradox that only the sinless can effect repentance for sinners. Or, to avoid the rather vague and bland double negative involved in speaking of sinlessness, only someone who is as completely attentive and committed to his Father's purpose as Jesus knows what needs to be done to condemn sin by making an end of it and to make a way out of the death of sin by which sinners can be put right with God. It is repentance (*metanoia*) that makes the new humanity and our repentance is impossible for us but is made actual in his dying to sin and giving himself to God on the cross. The distinctiveness

and uniqueness of that turning round to God of our humanity
consummated on Calvary is a vital component of the once-for-all
character of his death.

(iii) Obedient Confession for Us

We have spoken of the intercession of Christ with McLeod
Campbell, and of his repentance with Moberly, but we now speak
with Forsyth of his dying as his *confession* not simply in word but
in action of God's holy love.

Forsyth repeats in terms of confession what we have already
said in terms of repentance: 'The only adequate confession of a
holy God is a perfectly holy man.'[12] Jesus does not confess sin,
because only someone who has committed it can confess it.
Nevertheless in identification with sinners, he confesses the holy
love of God that condemns sin. By his reflecting back to the
Father his own holy love, he turns the cross – the place where
humanity is justly abandoned to the violent hatred and destructiveness it has chosen – into the place where God can look and see
his own holy love offered on our behalf. Thus Christ crucified
becomes the embodiment of the new humanity that is reconciled
to the Father in love and obedience. The conversion that he has
brought about in his own humanity becomes the pledge and the
promise of the conversion that he will work in ours. 'You must
think of the cross as setting up a new covenant and a new
humanity, in which Christ dwells as the new righteousness of
God.'[13] 'This is the taking of sin away – the acknowledgement
of judgement as holy, wise and good, and its conversion into
blessing; the absorption and confession of judgement into confession and praise, the removal of that guilt which stood between
God and man's reconciliation – the robbing sin of its power to
prevent communion with God.'[14]

Thus Jesus is seen as the intercessor who opens and submits to
God a human situation that has been closed and hostile to him.
He is seen as the one who works *metanoia*-repentance by turning
our humanity back to God, as one who from the depths of sin
confesses the holiness of the Father so that the Son as man on
earth and the Holy Father in heaven are in perfect correspon-
dence with each other.

All this Jesus does for us. He does not do for us what cannot
justly be done by any other. He is not unjustly punished for other

people's sins, he does not do penance for or make confession of sins he has not committed. But in profound unity with sinners and as one who sees far more clearly than we can what sin entails and what remedy it requires, he enters our nature and our situation and fashions there a new humanity in order then to share it with us. It is, in contrast with what has gone before, a humanity that calls to God, turns to God, reflects back the love of God. In such a humanity he shows himself to be the man in whom God's covenant with us is at last fulfilled.

(f) Identification Involves Judgement

In all this we have been emphasising the positive and forward looking aspects of the atoning work of Christ in quite deliberate reaction to what has often been an over-concentration on its negative and backward looking aspects. But, of course, the negative is there also, the judgement of the world is indeed the drawing of all people to the Christ lifted up on the cross to die, but it is also the casting out of the prince of this world, of the dark powers of evil that have enslaved these very people and who have to be dealt with before people can be drawn to the new beginning in Jesus (John 12:31–2). Until the old is dealt with the new cannot be born.

Karl Barth puts it this way:

> [God] now wills and demands the fulfilment of the covenant, the new man who not only knows and recognises and actively gives it to be understood, but lives wholly and utterly by the fact that He belongs to God, that He is His man . . . He wills and demands the sacrifice of the old man . . . He wills and demands the setting aside of this man, his giving up to death, which is not fulfilled by merely giving up this or that, even the best he has. *God wills and demands the man himself, to make an end of him, so that the new man may have air and space for a new life.* He wills and demands that he should go through death to life.[15]

The death of Jesus is the creation of the new humanity through the death of the old. The presence of God the Son on the cross reveals the depth of the alienation between his Father and his crucifiers, representing as they do the whole human race. To people who are as they are and therefore do as they do, God, in the wrath that is the shadow side of his holy love, can only say No. The scene at Calvary is dark with their rejection of God and God's rejection of them as they crucify his Son and hammer nails into his covenant. Things are moving closer and closer to the rejection and dissolution of an Israel and a world that is so at odds with its God. So Jesus' solemn words to the women on the road to Calvary who were weeping for him: "'Daughters of Jerusalem, do not weep for me; weep for yourselves and for your children. For the time will come when you will say, 'Blessed are the barren women, the wombs that never bore and the breasts that never nursed!' Then they will say to the mountains, 'Fall on us!' and to the hills 'Cover us!'"' (Luke 23:28–30). This is a people, representing a world that is bound for death under the just judgement of its God.

Jesus, by hanging on the cross and interceding for their forgiveness, walks that road with them and comes to the death that is at the end of it before them. In bearing that death which is the just consequence of what they have become, he affirms and executes the judgement of the Father that the wages of sin is death. But that just judgement is executed in a totally unexpected way. The death of the old humanity that, if it had befallen us, would have been a dead end, becomes through the obedience and the reflection of God's gracious love in which Jesus dies, the birth of the new humanity. A humanity that has died to sin, that has left sin behind it, that is now not a covenant-breaking but a covenant-keeping humanity to which God in the same justice that says No to sinners can now say Yes.

It is this Yes that is executed on Easter morning when the new man, sin and death behind him, rises and lives. He has turned the death, that under the wrath of God is the penalty due to sin, a death that is *for sin*, into a death that in the gracious love of God is a death *to sin* and therefore the gateway to new life for him and then in him for us. The past is abolished not by being compensated for but by being destroyed: Christ takes the sinful humanity that belongs to that past down with him to death so that it does not disrupt our relationship to God any more. It is destroyed by being sacrificed and the Priest of that sacrifice is the pioneer of the new humanity who will not die but live.

It is Forsyth who again shows best how the positive and the

negative, the prospective and the retrospective, hold together in the single act of his dying:

> For the holiness of God makes two demands: first for an answering holiness in love, and second, for a judgement on those who do not answer but defy. And Christ met both, in one and the same act. He was judged as one who, being made sin, was never sinful, but absolutely well-pleasing to God.[16]

3. The Gift of the New Humanity

At the Last Supper, pointing towards his death,[17] Jesus took bread and wine and by his word made them the effectuating signs of his body and his blood, himself and his life, his humanity. In the four actions of the sacrament we can see the four actions of Christ in relation to humanity. He *took* it, that is his incarnation and penetrated to the dark depths of it on the cross. He *blessed* it, he opened it up and offered it again to his Father so that it might be renewed in its relationship to him. He *broke* it, in his love and grace hung himself broken amidst all the sinful brokenness of the world that he might make common cause with us. He *gave* it, this assumed, broken and blessed humanity he brings from the cross and bids us eat and drink, and so receive his humanity into our own. So are God's new men and women born.

This humanity is the humanity of God and we must in the next chapter ask what it means to say that it was God the Son, of one being with the Father, who suffered and died on the cross.

7

One Cross – God on the Gallows

In the last chapter we were thinking of how, in Cardinal Newman's words, 'a second Adam to the fight and to the rescue came'. In Christ, however, Christian faith has always discerned not only the new humanity coming to birth amidst the condemnation and dissolution of the old, but the presence and action of the eternal Son of the living God. In the incarnation and therefore on the cross we encounter, according to another verse of the same hymn, 'God's presence and his very self'.

If this is so, it is of the highest relevance to our central concern in this book. The cross is distinctive not only because of the new kind of man who hung there, but because on it the living God himself suffered and died for his people and for his world. To quote Cardinal Newman again, we praise not just, with Jews and Muslims, the holiest who is in the height, but the holiest who is in the depth as well.

That is what Emil Brunner fifty years ago called the Scandal of Christianity. From the beginning, as Paul soon discovered, sophisticated Greeks rejected the whole idea of a crucified God as sheer folly and Jews, concerned for the divine sovereignty and greatness, counted it little less than blasphemy. Even Christian theologians down the centuries have often found it hard to cope with. It is difficult in all conscience to conceive of the mighty Creator becoming small enough for a cradle. It is still harder to think how he might have become vulnerable enough to suffer and die on a cross, let alone how the All Holy, who is of purer eyes than to behold iniquity, might be reduced to the obloquy and shame of a criminal execution.

1. The Crucifixion of God

(a) Biblical Evidence

And yet, if we are to be faithful to the New Testament gospel, that is exactly what we must say. In all the main New Testament sources it is either hinted or explicitly stated that on Calvary Sovereignty suffered and Deity died.

In Mark, Jesus, within hours of his execution, is questioned by the high priest: "'Are you the Christ, the Son of the Blessed One?" "I am, *(Ego eimi)*" said Jesus. "And you will see the Son of Man sitting at the right hand of the Mighty One and coming on the clouds of heaven." The high priest tore his clothes. "Why do we need any more witnesses?" he asked. "You have heard the blasphemy'" (Mark 14:61–4). Jesus' acceptance of the titles Son of the Blessed and Son of Man may legitimately be interpreted simply as assertions of his Messiahship. The *Ego eimi*, however, echoing as it does the divine 'I am' of Exodus 3:14, is an unambiguous claim to the divine name and divine identity and is so understood by Caiaphas as he denounces it as blasphemy. The man on the way to the cross claims not just to be serving God but to share his name and his nature. That claim is acknowledged after he has died by Mark's Roman centurion who has the last word: 'And when the centurion, who stood there in front of Jesus, heard his cry and saw how he died, he said, "Surely this man was the Son of God!"' (Mark 15:39). At the start and at the finish of his passion narrative Mark hints to those who have ears to hear that the man on the cross is God.

In Paul the hints in the gospel narrative become explicit statements. In the christological hymn in Philippians 2, the one who 'humbled himself and became obedient to death – even death on a cross' (2:8) is the one who has just been identified as being 'in very nature God' *(en morphe Theou)* (2:6). The connection in this passage between a very high Christology and the cross is all the more significant in that it comes at a very early stage of the theological development within the New Testament itself. From the start the Christian community was having its thinking about God and his nature decisively shaped by its encounter with the crucified and risen Jesus. As a result it was starting to think what apart from Jesus would have been unthinkable: that God's covenant love for his people was free not just to rule over them from on high, but, in complete consistency with itself, to become one of them, to express itself and fulfil its purposes in human obedience, human suffering and human death. If Philippians 2:1–11 is an early Christian hymn, this is what set them singing – the God who plunged from the heights to the depths to find his people; there is no name in heaven or on earth higher than this, the crucified is Lord.

Paul comes at the same point from a different direction in 2 Corinthians 5, when he is asking who is the ultimate agent of the reconciliation that Christ has made for us. He concludes that the agent of the new creation, as of all creation, is God himself. God did not send an agent other than himself to bring about our reconciliation but in Christ undertook it himself. Therefore, if anyone is in Christ, he is a new creation; the old has gone, the new has come! *All this is from God,* who reconciled us to himself through Christ and gave us the ministry of reconciliation: that God was *in Christ* reconciling the world to himself, not counting men's sins against them. And he has committed to us the message of reconciliation (2 Cor. 5:17–19).

Ultimately it takes a Trinitarian doctrine of God to clarify the relationships implicit in this passage. On the one hand the distinction between God and Christ as the originator and executor of the act of reconciliation is preserved throughout. At the same time God is seen as himself actively engaged in the act of reconciliation: 'God was in Christ (*ho theos en en Christo*) reconciling . . .' To reconcile is not the act of a third party distinct from God fulfilling the divine purpose, but as Christ's act is also God's act, implying the unity in being and yet the distinction in person between Father and Son that is expressed in later Trinitarian theology.

We can discern what is basically the same pattern in the Letter to the Hebrews. From the very start the one who will later be identified as the High Priest who purifies us from sin by his offering of himself is introduced as God's 'Son, whom he appointed heir of all things, and through whom he made the universe. The Son is the radiance of God's glory and the exact representation of his being, sustaining all things by his powerful word. After he had provided purification for sins, he sat down at the right hand of the Majesty in heaven' (Heb. 1:2–3). He who learned obedience through the things that he suffered and

poured out his blood to the death belongs to the being and is
involved in all the foundational acts of God.

When we turn to John this high Christology of the cross
becomes quite explicit, not least in John 3:16 where the Father is
compared to Abraham who is ready to sacrifice his only son,
Isaac, who is flesh of his flesh. So God gives up 'his only begotten
Son', being of his own being, divine with his own deity, in his
love for the world.

It is at the end of this gospel and in the immediate context of
the risen Jesus inviting Thomas to verify the wounds that were
made on the cross that the ultimate New Testament confession of
the deity of Jesus is made. 'Then he said to Thomas, "Put your
finger here; see my hands. Reach out your hand and put it into
my side. Stop doubting and believe." Thomas said to him, "My
Lord and my God!"' (John 20:27–8). No doubt it is the resurrection that *reveals* his divinity, but it only reveals what has been real
from the first and was real though still hidden on the cross. G. B.
Caird acknowledges that it was the resurrection that was the first
great growing point in the disciples thinking about Jesus:

> ... but what mattered was that it was the resurrection *of
> the crucified*. It was the work which they believed had been
> accomplished on the Cross which set them to asking the
> question. Who could have accomplished such a great work?
> By what right has he done it?[1]

The well-attested New Testament answer to these questions, is, as
we have seen, that he did it and had the right to do it because he
was, in being and action, one with God.

(b) Some Theological Questions

Having established our biblical basis we now need to go on and
ask our theological questions. What difference does it make to us
to see the suffering and dying of Jesus on Calvary as the suffering
and the dying of the Son of God? How are we to understand, on
the one hand, the essential unity and, on the other, the personal
differentiation of Father, Son and Holy Spirit in relation to what
was happening on the cross?

We need to affirm with John that the Father and the Son are one

but we need to do it in a way that just as strongly affirms, with
Mark and Matthew, the stark reality of the Son's god-forsakenness, on which his identification with us as the victims and
perpetrators of evil depends. He can reach the abandoned only if
he is himself abandoned, but he can bring God's liberating grace
fully into that situation only if he himself is fully God.

To say that of course only serves to raise still more questions.
What can it mean to say that the sovereign God becomes the
victim of evil, and still more what can it mean to say the living
God dies? Here if anywhere we are in the midst of mystery and
we must not pretend to know what we cannot know. As John
Heywood Thomas puts it: 'The greatest mystery is God's presence in Christ in his dying and in his death.'[2] Nevertheless it
belongs to our worship of the Crucified that we should survey
the wondrous cross from every angle we can, not indeed to dis-
solve or penetrate its mystery, but, as best we can to locate it and
to say what kind of mystery it is. So we can say that it is the
mystery of the crucified Son's unity with and separation from
the Father, and it is the mystery of the Holy Spirit's relating of the
one to the other. We look at each in turn.

2. The Son's Unity with the Father on the Cross

The cross of Christ involves the mystery of the crucified Son's
unbroken unity with the Father. It is in the last discourses in
the upper room that Jesus responds to Philip's request to see the
Father with the astounding assertion of their unity. Jesus
answered: "'Don't you know me, Philip, even after I have been
among you such a long time? Anyone who has seen me has seen
the Father. How can you say, "Show us the Father"? Don't you
believe that I am in the Father, and that the Father is in me? The
words I say to you are not just my own. Rather, it is the Father,
living in me, who is doing his work"' (John 14:9–11).

Where Jesus is present, the Father is also present; where Jesus is
at work, the Father is also at work; and that surely includes the
culminating and decisive work of atonement that is to happen
the next day on the cross. It is of course true that it is the Son and
not the Father who is crucified on Calvary and that distinction
has to be maintained if the self-offering of the Son to the Father is

to make any sense. But as the Son by his sacrifice offers himself
from the depths to the heights to the Father, so the Father from
the heights to the depths identifies himself with his Son. That
mutual self-offering and identification of the one with the other is
realised in the Spirit, who is indeed the Father's presence on the
Son's side of the relationship as he is also the Son's presence on
the Father's side of the relationship.[3] It is the Spirit who, as it
were, spans the infinite distance between heaven and Golgotha;
who spans the gulf that sin, suffering and death open between
them and makes the two one. As John V. Taylor puts it:

> What was the Holy Spirit doing at Calvary? First, in a
> mystery that we cannot plumb, he must have been about his
> eternal employ between the Father and the Son, holding each
> in awareness of the other, in an agony and bliss of love that
> must for ever lie infinitely beyond our understanding.[4]

That oneness of the Father and the Son in the Spirit is of central
importance to us for several reasons:

(a) Their Unity Guarantees Authentic Revelation

It assures us that Jesus on the cross is the ultimate expression of
the nature and character of God. There are medieval altarpieces
that depict the Father holding out in front of him the cross on
which his Son hangs. God is defined by his crucified Son, who
can represent his Father to us faithfully and definitively because
he is of the same being and nature. As Matthew puts it: 'No one
knows the Father except the Son and those to whom the Son
chooses to reveal him' (Matt. 11:27).

This was what was at stake in the Arian controversies of the
fourth century. If the Son was, as Arius taught, simply a creature,
however exalted, then his word and his actions lost their ultimacy and finality. Behind him lurked threateningly the ultimate
mystery of the inaccessible Godhead, unmoved and unmoving,
incapable in his static perfection of loving or taking decisive
action on behalf of his people. In such a scenario the cross of
Christ clearly loses its decisive significance; the love of Jesus is
only the love of a brother and not the love of God and the cross
gives no reliable clue about the nature of God's relationship with

his people. Against all that Paul affirms: 'God demonstrates *his own love (ten heautou agapen)* for us in this: While we were still sinners, Christ died for us' (Rom. 5:8). Such a statement makes sense only on the basis of a full identity in nature and character between Jesus and God.

The statement of the Nicene Creed that the Son is *homoöusios*, of one being with the Father, may sound remote and philosophical but it is in fact of the highest soteriological significance. As T. F. Torrance puts it:

> Since Jesus Christ, the only-begotten Son of God is of one being with the Father, and since he is God and man insepar-ably united in his incarnate Person, then like the incarnation, the atoning work of the incarnate Son falls within the inner life of the Holy Trinity ... The cross is not only a revelation of the love of Christ but a revelation of the love of God. The cross is a window opened into the very heart of God.[5]

This affirmation of the *homoöusion* means that Jesus' gracious will to forgive his enemies that brings him to the cross is a faithful reflection of the Father's unconditional will for reconciliation; that the grace of the Lord Jesus Christ is the efficacious irruption into history of the eternal love of God (2 Cor. 13:14). It means that God is not remote and inactive in the contemplation of his own perfection but dynamic in that initiating and costly love for his people. The love that comes seeking and saving that which is lost in Jesus is the hidden divine strategy that is secretly at work throughout human history. It means that the divine purpose cannot be achieved by the naked exercise of violent divine power, but only by identification with sufferers and sinners in a way that liberates them from the destructive past and opens them to and transforms them for a creative future. It means that what judges the world is the very love with which Jesus loved it from the cross. It is a love which on the one hand refuses to compromise itself with the suffering and the sin that contradicts and opposes it, but on the other hand goes to the length of ultimate self-offering to bring the sinners and the sufferers back to itself. It is a unity of will and purpose between Father and Son that the gospel of the cross presupposes and the gospel of the resurrection con-firms. It is on this identity between the act of Jesus and the purpose of the Father that all our Christian confidence depends.

(b) Their Unity Affirms the Father's Love

The affirmation of the *homoöusion* in relation to the cross rejects any view of atonement which presents us with a loving Jesus paying off an implacable God, or any view of the intercession of Christ as persuading a reluctant Father to forgive. As the Johannine Jesus himself declares to his disciples: 'In that day you will ask in my name. I am not saying that I will ask the Father on your behalf. No, *the Father himself loves you* because you have loved me and have believed that I came from God' (John 16:26–7). We can be confident in our approach to *Abba* only because we believe that Jesus is the definitive revelation of *Abba* and the love that he shows us in his death is the love that has its source in *Abba*. That is why it is the Spirit of his crucified Son that God sends into our hearts crying *Abba*, Father (Gal. 4:6).

(c) Their Unity Emphasises a Cosmic Atonement

The affirmation of the Father's involvement by the Spirit in the cross of the Son emphasises the cosmic over the merely pious and personal dimensions of Christ's deed on the cross. This is not a matter of entering into a cosy individual relationship with Jesus, as so much evangelical piety and indeed charismatic hymnody has often suggested, but rather the decisive act of the Creator God in confronting and overcoming the disruptive forces that are frustrating his purpose. That purpose, as Ephesians insists, is not just to 'save souls for heaven', but

> In him [Christ] we have redemption through his blood, the forgiveness of sins, in accordance with the riches of God's grace that he lavished on us with all wisdom and understanding. And he made known to us the mystery of his will according to his good pleasure, which he purposed in Christ, to be put into effect when the times will have reached their fulfilment – *to bring all things in heaven and on earth together under one head, even Christ.* (Eph. 1:7–10)

The cross is the act of the Creator by which he purposes not just a new kind of humanity but *kaine ktisis,* a whole renewed creation (2 Cor. 5:17), of which the Christian community is the sign, the foretaste and the promise. As Colossians puts it: 'For God was pleased to have all his fullness dwell in him, and through him to reconcile to himself all things, whether things on earth or things in heaven, by making peace through his blood, shed on the cross' (Col. 1:19–20). The cosmic divine purpose stretches out from the dying man on Calvary, through the community that believes in him, towards the creation of a new humanity and so affects and renews every nook and cranny of the created universe, transforming it into the new heavens and the new earth.

(d) The Cross as an Event in the Life of God

But, central to our own concern, the identity of the crucified Jesus with the Father indicates that the event of the cross is not just unique and distinctive for us, but it is unique and distinctive for God, Father, Son and Holy Spirit also. God is present and active in his world in all sorts of ways before the incarnation of his Son and in places and among people who have no knowledge of the crucifixion of Jesus of Nazareth and its saving import for them and for the world. However the ability to recognise and appreciate fully and fruitfully his presence and action in all these other times, places and people, depends on our discernment of his presence and action in the life, death and resurrection of Jesus Christ. It is there that his purpose and his character are finally revealed; there also that we are healed of the blindness and alienation from him that prevent us from discerning him elsewhere. When however we know Christ we can then begin to discern his presence and action everywhere. That presence is unique and distinctive in its incarnational identity with our humanity, culminating in his identification with our suffering and the consequences of our sin on the cross. For that reason, his presence and action in Jesus incarnate and crucified are normative for all discernment of his presence and action elsewhere.

To say the same thing in Johannine language, we can trace the footsteps of the Logos 'by whom all things were made' only when we have beheld the glory of the Logos who was made flesh and who is full of grace and truth. None of us has seen God directly and immediately, but the only-begotten Son who is in the bosom of the Father has made him known (John 1:1–17).

On the cross there is a two-fold sacrifice; on the one hand the costly self-offering of the Son to the Father on behalf of humanity, and on the other the self-offering of the Father in the giving of his Son to save the world. Paul and John both think of the Father's sacrifice of the Son in terms of Abraham's sacrifice of Isaac, an event that first threatens and then secures the future of Israel. Such a thought, as we have already seen, lies behind John 3:16 where the greatness of the Father's love for the world is proved by his willingness to give his only Son. It is expressed even more explicitly by Paul in Romans 8:32: 'He [God] did not spare his only Son but gave him up (*paredoken*) for us all.' He 'handed over' his Son to identify himself with those whom, according to Romans 1, he had already 'handed over' to the consequences of their own sinful choices – the verbs are the same in both passages.

In the incarnation and supremely on the cross God relates to humanity and through it to his whole creation in a way that he has never done before. He has always loved it but in this man and at this point in history that love expresses itself in a way it has never done before. The glory that consisted in the sovereign acts of creation and providence has become the incarnate glory that exposes itself to suffering and the consequences of human sin. The sympathy of the creator with his victimised human creatures moves into the empathy of the suffering fellow victim who is exposed to the injustice of human courts, the murdering violence of those whom his coming has threatened, the hatred of enemies, the desertion of friends, the agony of unrelieved physical pain, mental anguish and spiritual desolation. He who has always been the Judge of all the earth now fulfils his promise himself to take responsibility for the human situation that is slowly disintegrating under that judgement. He takes the old humanity in its alienation down to death and in himself raises up the new humanity to life.

All this, by his will and purpose, happens to God who is Father and Son. On the cross outside Jerusalem, when Pontius Pilate is governor of Judaea, God suffers; God is among the god-forsaken; God dies. This has never happened before and will never happen again. There can be no possibility of or need for another incarnation because the Son of God who is the new man lives for ever with his Father. There can be no possibility of or need for another crucifixion, because the self-offering of the cross which is historically past is perpetually present and for ever powerful in all God's dealings with humanity; the great High Priest for ever

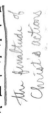

the finititude of Christ's actions

offers his once-made sacrifice at the right hand of the Father. The cross is unique and distinctive for us because first of all it is unique and distinctive for God. It is, as T. F. Torrance says, not only a decisive action in history, but also a pivotal moment in the relation of Father and Son in the inner life of God, on which all his dealings with us before and after depend.

(e) The Cross Reshapes our Ideas about God

If the crucified Jesus is of the same being with God, then we have to allow our ideas about God to be reshaped by what he shows us of him on the cross. If we come to Calvary with preconceived notions about God's nature, we shall not be able rightly to recognise him in what happens there. How can a God who is decked out with a host of attributes that begin with '*omni*' or '*im*' – who is omniscient, omnipotent etc. – ever become incarnate, let alone crucified? How can a God who is defined as being immutable, impassible and immortal, incapable of change, of suffering at the hands of others and unable to die, ever be involved in the suffering that Jesus endured and the death he died at Calvary?

These are very real questions but the theological tradition has often got into unnecessary tangles in its attempts to answer them. This is because it has been working with definitions of the divine nature that have their source in philosophical systems that see God in terms of static self-sufficient and absolute being, rather than as the God who reveals himself in the story of Israel and the coming of Jesus.

It is because such an absolutist model heavily influences it that Islamic theology sees Christian talk about the suffering and death of God in Christ as intolerable blasphemy. Even Christian theologians have been reduced to saying that Jesus suffered and died in his human but not in his divine nature. This results in a schizophrenic understanding of his person that finds it hard to answer unambiguously the question: The Son of God, did he or did he not suffer and die?

If however we allow our understanding of the nature of God to be shaped, not by a philosophy whose concepts we then impose upon it, but by God's historical self-revelation that culminates in the incarnation and atoning work of Jesus, we shall be able, not to provide complete answers to these questions, but to tackle them in a different and more biblical perspective.

I find Karl Barth's understanding of God as the one who loves in freedom particularly helpful at this point:[6] God is free to do what his love purposes. His immutability consists not in his inability to change, but in his faithfulness to his loving purposes. His omnipotence is not an imprisoning greatness, but his freedom to do whatever his loving purpose requires. It is to be free to be great or to be small, to be strong or to be weak, to know everything or to share human ignorance. It is to be free to be born as a man, to suffer as a man and to die as a man on a cross. That is not the abnegation of his power, it is his exercising of it in a new way in which his love purposes to restore and renew his creation.

He is impassible only in the sense that nothing in his creation can compel him or force his hand. In freedom he comes to us and accepts the constraints and limitations of our humanity. In freedom he plunges to the depths of our suffering. In freedom he walks the way of death. No man takes his life from him. In his freedom he lays it down for us; that is what gives his suffering and death its saving efficacy because in it he freely expresses his love to his Father and to his world. It remains totally wonderful and utterly mysterious that the Creator should go that far to seek and save his fallen creation, but it is not the miracle of metaphysical paradox but the miracle of God's free and gracious love.

3. The Son's Separation from the Father on the Cross

We have been looking at some of the ways in which our understanding of the cross is shaped by the basic Christian belief in the divinity of Jesus and in so doing we have been stressing the unity of nature, the *homoöusion* of the Father and the Son in the Spirit, in Johannine terms, 'The Father and I are one' (John 10:30).

But we must now come to terms with the fact that that unity is threatened and perhaps even disrupted by what happens to Jesus on the cross. Between this Father and this Son who are one in being and nature, there come first the god-forsakenness and then the death that are the consequences of evil, whether as inflicted suffering or self-destructive sin. All evil is separation from God and Jesus on the cross so identified himself with the victims and the perpetrators of evil that he shares this separation, and cries from the midst of his agony, 'My God, my God, why have you forsaken me?' This, according to Moltmann, signifies 'the total, inextricable abandonment of Jesus by his God and Father'[7] because only if he stands completely on the same ground as the victims and the villains is he able to help them. But in such total abandonment, what then becomes of his unity with God?

Before we address that question we have to see that just at this point there is another and, at first sight, contradictory side to the biblical witness. In the final discourses in John Jesus, contemplating the desertion of the disciples says: 'But a time is coming, and has come, when you will be scattered, each to his own home. You will leave me all alone. *Yet I am not alone, for my Father is with me*' (John 16:32). Some commentators think that this may indeed be a deliberate Johannine riposte to the Markan cry of desolation. However that may be, they are both part of the scriptural evidence about what was happening to the Father–Son relationship when Jesus died on the cross.

McLeod Campbell, who is nervous of the cry of desolation because he sees it as providing support for a penal theory of atonement, makes much of the Johannine correction and suggests, as others have done since, that we should take seriously the fact that the cry of desolation is the first verse of Psalm 22. He wants us to recognise that Jesus has the whole psalm in mind and is moving with it from the desolation at the beginning to the hope and expectancy at the end. I have never found this very convincing and it looks suspiciously like an attempt to evade the awful implications of the Son's abandonment by the Father on the cross.

What then shall we say? We need to be very careful at this point not to try to go beyond the evidence and to intrude into the silence of the crucified Jesus by attributing to him thoughts and reactions that belong to a divine mystery that is far beyond our ken. Nevertheless both the Markan and the Johannine strands of the tradition are to be taken with utter seriousness and we must not play down one in favour of the other. Jesus' unity with the Father, and his penetration into the world of sin, suffering and death that are bound for destruction because they are separated from the Father – both these factors are at the centre of the saving power of the cross. How can we affirm both?

(a) Unbroken Unity of Purpose

We can of course say that the Son in his abandonment and the Father in his glory are both one, because they are each pursuing in ways that are appropriate to them the one divine purpose for the liberation of the victims from their suffering and the sinners from their sin. The Father in the giving of his Son and the Son in his self-offering to the Father are both acting in the freedom of the divine love that they both share. The Father so loves the world that he gives his Son; the Son so loves the sufferers and the sinners that he freely gives himself to them and for them.

Furthermore Father and Son, each in his different way, are both involved in the suffering, the Son as the one who bears it, and the Father as the one who, for the sake of his love for the world, has to abandon his Son to it. As Hans Urs von Balthasar puts it: 'He who is thus handed over is, in the truest sense of the word, abandoned by God. God ceases to dispose of him, and his enemy does so instead.'[8] That the Father, in pursuit of his loving purpose, should cease to dispose of his beloved Son but hand him over to his sinful human destroyers and the powers of spiritual wickedness that lurk behind them is indeed suffering and grief – the grief of a voluntary helplessness that cannot intervene without disrupting the whole process of identification that the deliverance of sufferers and sinners requires. Moltmann speaks at this point of the mourning Father,[9] who, like all mourners for the dying, has to watch and let the whole dire process take its course.

(b) Abandonment is not Dissolution of Relationship

Nevertheless we may ask if Moltmann goes too far when he insists that the god-forsakenness of Jesus implies not just his abandonment to the power of his enemies, but the total if temporary disruption of the Father–Son relationship. 'The grief of the Father is just as important here as the death of the Son. The Fatherlessness of the Son is matched by the Sonlessness of the Father, and if God has constituted himself as the Father of Jesus Christ, then he also suffers the death of his Fatherhood in the death of the Son.'[10] Is the abandonment on the cross the way to the dissolution of the Father–Son relationship in death?

(c) The Father's Presence with the Son in the Spirit

It is at this point that the Markan emphasis on the separation between Father and Son has to be corrected by the Johannine emphasis on their continuing together. Jesus abandoned to the power of his enemies is not left alone in that dire situation, because even there his Father, who will not intervene to end the suffering, is yet with him in the suffering.

I want to put it this way: on the cross the Son is not with the Father, but on the cross the Father is still with the Son. Jesus in the agony of his suffering and in his sharing of the separation from God that is the consequence of sin can no longer realise or affirm that togetherness with the Father that has been at the centre of his life. The affirmatory moments when he is affirmed as Son in his baptism and his transfiguration have given way to a closed and silent heaven from which the divine presence has been totally withdrawn and the divine purpose can longer be grasped. All that is clearly implied in his despairing cry, 'My God, my God, why have you forsaken me?'

The Father in his own person, in the pursuit of his loving purpose, remains withdrawn from the Son and does nothing to relieve him. But the bond between Father and Son is the person of the Holy Spirit. The Spirit is the Father's presence on the Son's side of the relationship. In his own person the Father is distinct from the Son, but in the Spirit he gives himself to the Son in the way that is appropriate to the Son's situation at the different stages of his calling. In the Jordan, the affirmation of Sonship is accompanied by a renewed donation of the Spirit in a way that is appropriate to the ministry then beginning.

On the cross, even when he has no sense of communion or communication with the Father, the Spirit of the Father is not withdrawn from the Son. As we have already seen it is from the cross with his work done that he hands over the Spirit to his disciples and, as we shall see in a moment, it is in the Spirit that he offers himself on our behalf to the Father. So, though in his own person the Father is withdrawn from the Son, in the Spirit he is still with the Son on Calvary, in the mutual interpenetration of the Trinitarian persons that constitutes their unity. The mutuality of the Father–Son relationship is broken, but the unifying and sustaining gift of the Spirit by the Father to the Son remains.

(d) The Spirit of Faithful Endurance

The Father's Spirit is present with the suffering and dying Son in a way that is appropriate to his abandonment to suffering and the consequences of sin. He is there in a way that does not destroy his identification with us but that enables him to cope with it. He can be present there not as the ecstatic Spirit of Pentecost but as the reticent Spirit of patient endurance (*hupomone*), who does not stage dramatic deliverances but enables the Son to travel through his sufferings in trust and hope in his apparently absent and unresponding Father. In Paul's list of the fruit of the Spirit in Galatians (5:22) love, joy and peace are followed by patience, which does not mean passive resignation, but rather courageous endurance in the midst of trouble. This patient endurance is inspired by God and is his gift to his people when they are under unrelieved pressure. So in Colossians the writer prays for the members of that church that they may be 'strengthened with all power according to his glorious might, so that you may have great endurance and patience' (Col. 1:11). Such patient endurance comes from God in the Spirit and it is the gift that is appropriate to the Son in the abandonment of the cross.

The Spirit inspires the endurance that enables the Son in his abandonment still to cling and cry to the Father. Thus the relationship between them is not dissolved at the cross but affirmed in a way that is appropriate to the cross. When Jesus cries, 'My God, my God, why have you forsaken me?' it is indeed the cry of a bewildered man who can no longer make sense of what has happened to him and who has lost his closeness to his Father and his mission. This is the only recorded prayer of his that does not begin with the word Father. Its starting point is indeed that of a god-forsaken man.

But there is more to it than that. It is no longer confident prayer to the Father, but it is still prayer; it is still addressed to 'my God'. It is the prayer of one who is still trusting when every ground of trust has been removed, it asks a question that expects an answer, it refuses to abandon God even when it seems that God has abandoned him. It is the prayer of Job: 'Though he slay me, yet will I hope in him' (Job 13:15). It is by that prayer that the desolate Son expresses and maintains in the Spirit his relationship with the Father and opens up that dire situation to the God who is able to transform and renew it and will soon do so, as he raises his Son from the dead.

Paul Fiddes does not approve of attempts to interpret the cry of desolation in this positive way and he criticises the liberation theologian, Boff, for adopting it: 'This breach in God cannot be diminished, even by saying with Boff that Jesus turns his deepest despair into "trust in the Mystery". The cry of forsakenness cannot be abridged like this; it is not resolved at the cross into a word of trust but rings out in all its starkness.'[11] To insist in that way on Jesus' sense of desolation 'in all its starkness' as the only dominating factor in his relationship with God on the cross is not only to ignore the work of the Spirit, but it is to fail to do justice to the total witness of the gospels which insist that Jesus died in trust and hope in his Father. One might even ask Fiddes what, on his showing, there was about Jesus in his death that made the centurion hail him as Son of God.

It was indeed the expression of hope and trust in God that Jesus brought into the god-forsakenness that he shared, that enables him to bring the same hope and trust to other sufferers and that singles him out from all the other victims who went to death in unrelieved despair. Boff's phrase about his turning despair into 'trust in the Mystery' is exactly appropriate. It was in trusting the Mystery that God had become that Jesus in the patient endurance of the Spirit maintained and affirmed his eternal relationship with the Father. It was this that enabled him to give himself to the Father on the cross.

We might almost say that the pattern that Paul holds out to us in Romans 5 is the pattern of what was going on with Jesus on the cross: 'We know that suffering produces perseverance; perseverance, character; and character, hope. And hope does not disappoint us, because God has poured out his love into our hearts by the Holy Spirit, whom he has given us' (Rom. 5:3–5). It was the Spirit of the Father's love poured out in the Spirit on the Son – whom the Father had for that moment handed over to his enemies – that inspired in him the perseverance that called on God as 'My God' from the very depths into which he had fallen. It was the Spirit that brought him through to the hope that, according to Luke, finally enabled him to commend his life and his destiny into his Father's hands.

The involvement of the Spirit in the self-offering of the Son is further indicated in Hebrews: 'How much more, then, will the

Words on cross = big deal — if our working of God's forsakeness isn't big, then something wrong

blood of Christ, *who through the eternal Spirit (dia pneumatos aioniou) offered himself unblemished to God*, cleanse our consciences from acts that lead to death, so that we may serve the living God!' (Heb. 9:14). Although other interpretations are possible this has traditionally been taken as a reference to the Holy Spirit and as pointing to his activity at Calvary, doing and being in these unique circumstances what he eternally is and does. He has his being and his function in the relation of Father and Son to each other. Therefore, across the chasm of the Son's identification with the god-forsaken, he continues to mediate in the ways we have been suggesting: the sustaining self-giving of the Father to the Son, and the saving and purifying self-giving of the Son to the Father.

In this whole section we have been maintaining that within the framework of a Trinitarian doctrine of God, it is at least possible to hold together the Markan emphasis on Jesus' real identification with the victims and perpetrators of evil in their god-forsakenness and yet to maintain, with John, that even there, through the Spirit, the relationship of the Father with the Son and the relationship of the Son with the Father was maintained and expressed. It is on the affirmation of that relationship in precisely that situation that all the hopes of the victims and perpetrators of evil depend.

4. The Spirit and the Dead Son

If it is hard to understand how the Father–Son relationship is maintained when Jesus is among the god-forsaken, it is even harder to understand how it could be maintained when at the end of his passion he is among the dead. What can it possibly mean to say that the eternal Son of God has died? It is to that question that we must now turn, because it is clearly set before us by the credal and Trinitarian framework within which we are working. The Nicene creed within its second christological answer affirms that he of whom it speaks is 'of one Being (*homoöusios*) with the Father' and also that as part of his work 'for us men and our salvation', 'he suffered death and was buried', but it does not tell us how we are to understand these statements in their relationship to each other.

Hans Urs von Balthasar warns against failing to face up to the stark fact of Holy Saturday, the fact of a dead Christ. We can rush on too quickly to the joys of the third day; we can, with the Greek iconographers, picture a living and active and glorious Christ invading the world of the dead, raising Adam and Eve from their coffins in a pre-resurrection triumph. All that has its place, but it must not be allowed to displace or distract attention from the fact that from Good Friday to Holy Saturday the Son of God lies dead. His identification with us will be incomplete and his saving act insufficient if he does not share with us the ultimate consequence of our subservience to evil, either as its victims or its servants. Hebrews is quite clear that it belongs to the redeeming act of God's grace that Jesus should experience the death that all of us have to experience and that this is the way he must go in order to reach his glorious destination: '. . .we see Jesus, who was made a little lower than the angels, now crowned with glory and honour *because he suffered death, so that by the grace of God he might taste death for everyone*' (Heb. 2:9).

Death, whatever function it might be designed to fulfil in the purpose of the Creator, becomes for those who are the sinful victims of evil the dreaded ultimate moment in which the destructiveness that is endemic to the sinful situation finally has its way. When we die all our relationships with God and with people are severed and we are carried from being to non-being: 'The wages of sin is death.' Jesus dies, to quote Hebrews again, to 'free those who all their lives were held in slavery by their fear of death' (Heb. 2:15).

The illusion of death as the automatic transition from an imperfect to a perfect heavenly state, deceptively propagated at many semi-Christian funerals, is untrue both to scripture and experience. Death can be more biblically and realistically described as the 'ultimate enemy' (1 Cor. 15:26) and our reluctance to contemplate the reality of our own death only goes to prove the point.

There must therefore be no mitigation of the awfulness of death either in Jesus' case or our own. As von Balthasar puts it:

It [death] is a happening which affects the whole person, though not necessarily to the point of obliterating the human subject altogether. It is a situation which signifies in the first place the abandonment of all spontaneous activity and so a passivity, a state in which, perhaps, the vital activity now brought to an end is mysteriously summed up.[12]

Death is the collapse of all relationships into unresponsiveness. Those who are dead can neither speak nor be spoken to, they can neither receive love nor return it, they can neither initiate nor participate in all the activities and concerns in which our relationships are expressed and by which they are nourished. 'I have lost my husband', says the widow, and exactly that is the source of her grief. All that makes up life is lost to the dead and they are lost to it.

And so it is with Jesus, as his body is lowered from the cross and carried to Joseph of Arimathea's dark garden tomb. No more parables, no more healing, no more praying to his Father; he has offered everything and he has nothing more. It looks as if all the hopes he roused are now reduced to mocking illusions, his promises become retreating echoes fading into nothingness: The Son of God is dead.

As Alan Lewis puts it, we are 'compelled to confront the possibility that God's own Son is dead and buried among the transgressors, and that God himself has failed in his fatherhood and deity' and as a consequence 'the world is delivered up to godlessness and negativity'.[13] That is the reality of Holy Saturday and we must give it its own space and its own meaning before we hurry on to Easter Sunday, not least because Holy Saturday is a day that both individuals and the Church have to live through again and again. We shall all have to confront the day of our dying when resurrection may seem a distant hope rather than an imminent reality.

The Son of God is dead; his death is our death. It is an evil undoing of the work of the Creator which looks like the final triumph of all the powers of darkness that have brought him to the cross. He is dead and unresponsive to his friends and he is dead and unresponsive to his Father. This is the ultimate disruptive attack on the unity of Father and Son, this is the permitted intrusion of death into the Trinitarian life of God.

Nevertheless what we said above about his desolation holds true even here about his death. In his furthest absence from the Father, the dead Son is still in profound unity with the Father. His passivity and unresponsiveness are still the expressions of his obedience that hold him in oneness with the Father in his

unity = obedience
↳ almost sounds like process theology

execution of the Father's redeeming purpose. That fact alone
makes his death different from ours and, even before the resurrection, full of hope for ours. This dead man is indeed bearing the
death of the victims and perpetrators of evil, but he is bearing it
as the loved and obedient Son of the Father.

5. *The Distinct Personhood of the Spirit*

The self-giving love of the Father for the Son and of the Son for
the Father *is enacted in the Holy Spirit who is distinct from both of
them and holds them both together.* In that Spirit the Father holds his
dead Son still in his love even when the Son cannot receive or
respond to that love. And even when the Son is dead the Spirit
lives and goes on relating him to the Father even in his deadness,
because that deadness is the ultimate expression of his love and
goes on being offered in the Spirit when he can no longer offer it
for himself. So in the Spirit the Trinitarian union of Father and
Son is maintained not in spite of, but through the death that has
intruded into it. Even when it is expressed in the passivity of
death, the Son's attentive and obedient love for the Father by
which the worlds were made and are sustained is held fast by the
Spirit within the life of God.

It is at precisely this point that the distinctive nature of the
person and action of the Spirit over against the person and action
of the Son is of the greatest importance, as Alan Lewis has most
helpfully shown:

> No 'mere' bond of love between the Father and the Son, the
> Spirit is rather the active bond who holds Sender and Sent
> together in the Father's abandonment of the Son to death.
> And in that very death he holds the Creator and the creation
> together, securing God's even closer union with mortal
> sinners at the locus of their greatest distance.[14]

Thus in the death of the Son, the closed and dark realm of death,
our death, the death of the transgressors, is invaded by God and
held within his Trinitarian life, enfolded in the Father's love for
the Son and the Son's love for the Father in the Spirit. That is
why the realm of death cannot remain closed and dark for much

longer. It is soon broken open by the dead Son whose presence there is the ultimate expression of his obedience to the Father who is the source of life and who is joined up to that source by the Spirit who is the Lord and giver of life. Against such a saving coalition the gates of Hell cannot long prevail. When the Spirit follows the Son into the realm of darkness he soon makes himself known as the 'Spirit of him who raised Jesus from the dead' (Rom. 8:11). When that happens, it is Easter day.

In the death of Jesus the world of the dead is opened up to the Word of God who has entered it by dying; the death of Jesus has retrospective power for those who lived before it as well as prospective power for those who live after it. That is at least part of the meaning of the mysterious verses in 1 Peter that speak of how Jesus 'was put to death in the body but made alive by the Spirit, through whom also he went and preached to the spirits in prison' (1 Pet. 3:18–19, c.f. also 4:6); verses that are the source of the credal phrase 'He descended to the dead.'

Such high theology may seem speculative and daunting, but it is in fact only an attempt to set the fact of the death of Jesus in a Trinitarian setting that both allows it to be what it is and at the same time to show the basis on which it can be overcome when it is set within the context of the three-fold love of God. *don't think he is*

Pastorally and personally, it provides a basis for hopeful contemplation of our own deaths. When all responsiveness is impossible for us and there is nothing that we can do but surrender to the darkness, all the more dreadful when we realise it is deserved darkness, then with Christ and in Christ we can be held in the Holy Spirit within the love of God and brought through the *not taking* passivity of our holy Saturday, however long, to the new day *death* when the dead are raised and all things are made new. *seriously*

On the cross, the Son of God is on the gallows, desolate, deserted and then dead. But, in the awful reality of that, he is still held by the Spirit in his unity with the Father that will transform and overcome all. That our God has come this far for us and made a way from this distance back to himself – this is our gospel, our hope and our joy.

One Cross – Baptism into Communion

The work of the cross is completed: with his great cry of victory, 'Tetelestai – It is perfectly finished', Jesus hands over his Spirit to his Father above him in sacrifice, and to his disciples around him as the gift, pledge and promise of a new, forgiven and reconciled humanity.

On the third day the Father responds to the sacrifice with resurrection. In his risen glory Jesus turns back to his disciples and begins to involve them in the consequences of what he has done for them. Till now they have been excluded; the work done on the cross is his work and not theirs, and, whether they fled from it or watched him as he died, they have had no part in it. He has been to places where no one, however willing, can follow. So in John, when he speaks of his imminent departure, 'Simon Peter asked him, "Lord, where are you going?" Jesus replied, "Where I am going, you cannot follow now, but you will follow later"' (John 13:36–7). There is work to be done that none but he can do, a sacrifice to be made that none but he can offer, a death to be endured that none but he can die. This belongs to the distinctiveness of the cross that we have until now been expounding.

But post-resurrection, all that changes; the excluded are included, the disciples who either fled or mourned are now to be re-called, re-commissioned and involved in the whole process of their own re-making and the ultimate re-making of the world for which he has given himself. Mary Magdalene comes to anoint a dead body and finds herself summoned to turn from her preoccupation with death and the grave to come face to face with a living Jesus and to be caught up in his saving purposes. 'He said to her, "Mary" and she turned round to him and said Master"' (John 20:16). That is repentance indeed! The same evening the risen Christ who bears, as he will bear for ever, the marks of his crucifixion, breaks in on his disciples, reveals his presence, imparts his peace, breathes his Spirit and sends them out to declare and enact the release from the alienation of the past that he has won.

What he has done he has done alone, but he has done it on our behalf and for our sakes and it will have been done in vain unless we are affected by it and incorporated into it. But how does that come about? Moberly puts the question like this:

> How does it happen, by what power and by what means, that what is primarily an external fact consummated in history, can and does become the essential reality in the characterisation of the personalities of men? How can the sacrifice of Jesus Christ, consecrated on Calvary for eternal presentation become in me – not a personal reality only, but the main constitutive reality of my own individual personal being?[1]

That incorporation of his people into his completed work of atonement is the subject of this chapter and we cannot do better than approach it by looking at the two gospel sacraments which symbolise and effect that incorporation. To be baptised is to be initiated into that incorporation; to receive the Eucharist is to have that incorporation confirmed and renewed.

1. Two Sacraments of Incorporation

Both sacraments are what they are and effect what they effect only in relationship to the word of the gospel that they proclaim in visible symbol and eventful action. Their power is not in themselves but in the crucified and risen Christ who has appointed them and comes to his people through them. That work he does through the power of his spoken and enacted word to create and sustain faith in those who are exposed to it. To be incorporated into Christ is precisely to trust that what he has done for you has achieved a reconciled relationship with God that no act of your own could ever achieve, that the new humanity that lives in peace with God and with neighbour is, from start to finish, the gift of the crucified and has to be received again and again from his hand.

The sacraments are the highlighted moments of that receiving, that reveals its meaning and its nature to us. The presence of the risen Jesus was not confined to the supper table of the house in Emmaus. He had walked with them as an anonymous presence on the road. He has talked with them as a teaching presence in his word, so that their hearts had burned within them, yet they knew and received him as he really was when he took and blessed and broke and gave the bread. Our incorporation into Christ is not confined to special moments at the font or the altar; it is the spring and source of the living water that we drink every day, but it is at the font and the altar that the living Christ shows us who he is for us and what we are to receive from him and give to him. That is why we look to the sacraments, instituted by the spoken word of the incarnate Word, creating and renewing faith by the power of the Spirit, to reveal to us what it means to be incorporated into the death and resurrection of the Lord.

(a) Incorporation and Baptism

Our baptism marks the beginning of that incorporation. Paul is quite clear about that in Romans 6: 'Don't you know that all of us who were baptised into Christ Jesus were baptised into his death? We were therefore buried with him through baptism into death in order that, just as Christ was raised from the dead through the glory of the Father, we too may live a new life' (Rom. 6:3–4). As Jesus identified himself with our plight and our need for radical *metanoia*, repentance, in his own baptism in the Jordan, so in our baptism we are identified with him in his death to sin and his rising to a new life of right relationships with God and with people.

We should notice here that the movement in these verses is not from Christ to us but rather from us to Christ. It is not so much that his life and death are to be repeated or reproduced in our living and dying, but rather that by baptism we are to be included in his dying and living which are present and potent realities that are there waiting – or rather reaching out – for us and are therefore open and available to us. It is indeed true that his death and rising are past historical events that are once for all and have no need to be repeated. Paul is quite clear about that: 'For we know that since Christ was raised from the dead, he cannot die again; death no longer has mastery over him' (Rom. 6:9).

(b) The Contemporary Christ

But that event which is historically unrepeatable is perpetually available; the risen and ascended Jesus does not leave his passion behind him; he is defined by it and acts in the light of it for ever. We shall get the matter wrong if we think of the work of atonement as past and our experience as present, as though there were some great problem in spanning the gap of the centuries that divides us from it. The cross is indeed past, but the crucified is risen, he is for ever the man who has died to sin and lives to righteousness. As such he is perpetually our contemporary and to be baptised into him is to be incorporated into the present power and reality of his death and his resurrection.

The Letter to the Hebrews makes the same point in relation to Christ's sacrifice. The very document that emphasises the *eph' hapax*, the once and for all nature of that sacrifice, is equally clear that the sacrifice once made so perfectly that it is unrepeatable, is perpetually offered on our behalf in intercession to the Father: 'Because Jesus lives for ever, he has a permanent priesthood. Therefore he is able to save completely those who come to God through him, because he always lives to intercede for them' (Heb. 7:24–5). The great High Priest is our contemporary, so that through what he once did we can be purified and offered in him to the Father.

A clear implication of that is that the new humanity into which the ultimate Adam incorporates us by his Spirit is a contemporary and living humanity. We are not called upon to become messianic Jews of the first century, like the first apostles. In that Jewish culture, made ready for it down the centuries, that new humanity was forged and formed and it is indelibly marked by it for ever.

Jesus of Nazareth is for ever the Messiah of Israel or he is nothing at all. Everything that follows has to emerge from that and be consonant with that. But the humanity that came to its birth, its death and its rising in that culture is not the prisoner of that time or of any time. Coming from that culture it is able to relate to every culture and every other expression of humanity, in both judgement and fulfilment. Jesus Christ who is the same yesterday, today and for ever is for that very reason not just a man of the first century but a man of the twenty-first century. He is always in faithfulness to his Father and himself but always also in utter relevance to us and the issues that our culture sets before us, many of which the people of the first century, including the New Testament writers, were totally unaware of. The crucified and risen Lord is not just behind us calling us back, he is with us sending us out and ahead of us summoning us on. To be delivered from sin by his death and to be raised to life by his resurrection is to be liberated from the burdens of the past so that we can relate to the present and be ready for the future.

(c) Incorporation and the Eucharist

The same contrast between the historically unrepeatable and the presently available comes out in a different way in relation to the Eucharist. Here the movement is not, as in Paul's teaching on baptism in Romans, from us into Christ but from Christ into us. We are to eat of his body and drink of his blood so that what he is becomes what we are. The contrast is itself illuminating. Our incorporation is, in its initial baptismal enactment, a movement that takes us out of ourselves into the crucified and risen Jesus. The result is that, when and because we are in him by our baptism, he can be in us in the giving and receiving of the Eucharist. That second movement emphasises that his atoning work does in fact reach its goal in his people, that it has that intimate and personal dimension that Paul celebrates when he says: 'I have been crucified with Christ and I no longer live, but Christ lives in me. The life I live in the body, I live by faith in the Son of God, who loved me and gave himself for me' (Gal. 2:20–1).

The double emphasis on the once and for all historical action, on the one hand, and present communion on the other, is summed up in the command to 'do this in remembrance of me' and in the invitation to eat of his body and drink of his blood. We are to participate in the new humanity that has been offered in sacrifice on our behalf in the midst of the old crucifying humanity, so that the one may overcome the other in us. We receive his body and are therefore, in the literal meaning of the word, incorporated into him and into the people who belong to him. The sacrament is, as remembrance of the redemptive act in the past, well described as the Lord's Supper; in relation to the sharing of his death and life in the present it is the Holy Communion, and as receptive response to both it is the Eucharist, the Thanksgiving.

My old teacher, John Baillie, used to say that our relationship to God in Christ involved what he called a 'mediated immediacy'.[2] This phrase helps us to understand the relationship between the past historical act and the living presence of the crucified Jesus, on which, as we have been seeing, both sacraments in their different ways depend. Our relationship to Christ is a mediated one. We have no direct hot-line to the right hand of God; our knowledge of the crucified and risen Lord comes to us through his incarnation at a certain time and place in human history and the witness of those who met him then. To know anything of his atoning work, we have to do what we have been doing throughout this book and expose ourselves to what happened there and then, once and for all on Calvary and on Easter morning, and search the multifaceted presentations and interpretations of the paschal event that the New Testament writers offer us. Our knowledge of Christ is from beginning to end dependent on that kind of mediation. If we do not remember him in his history, we shall not be able to eat of his body or drink of his blood.

Nevertheless the invitation so to eat and drink, so to enter into a present one-to-one relationship with Christ as we share in the communion of his people, is itself the sign of the ongoing miracle of the Church's life whereby what is a historically and scripturally mediated relationship becomes again and again a present I – Thou relationship, a present dealing, an exchange of life with a risen Lord. A communion service that is seen only in terms of historical remembering can easily become a gloomy memorial service for a remote and long dead Jesus. One has even seen holy tables behind which, in an excess of misplaced Protestant zeal, is written the totally inappropriate legend, 'He is not here, he is risen', against which the modern Anglican rites very properly protest, 'The Lord is here. His Spirit is with us.' The glory of it is that the reality of the presence often breaks through despite the restrictions of a merely memorialist theology and the communicants do know that their lives have been touched again by a living and present Lord. Through the remembering, the presence:

through the mediated, the immediacy. It is, as we shall see, because his Spirit is indeed with us, that it continues to be so.

The Church, then, goes on remembering the Jesus of history because it has an expectation grounded in long experience of encountering the Christ of today. What was done at the cross without us and for us long ago becomes effective in us as we are incorporated into the crucified living of the Lord who has made an end of sin and a way through suffering and death into a new humanity that knows and responds to the Father's love and itself mediates that love to others. If that stopped happening the Church would die, because the Church cannot live on its history but only out of its constantly renewed incorporation into and communion with its Lord.

2. *The Vicarious Christ*

The question of our relationship to what Christ has done for us on the cross has often been discussed in terms of whether his action on our behalf is best described as substitutionary, representative or vicarious. This is another of these terminological minefields that have often been laid in the territory of atonement theology. Not only is it unclear what exactly is meant by different writers when they describe Christ as our substitute, our representative or the one who acts vicariously on our behalf, but each of the terms has flourished in a particular context and has been adopted as a combative battle-cry, not to say shibboleth, to defend one approach and to repudiate others. Furthermore it is far from certain that any of the terms involved is adequate to its subject matter. John McIntyre in his excellent discussion of this whole matter brings some light into this confused situation,[3] first by pointing to the theological provenance from which each of the terms comes. Those who promote penal theories of atonement are most happy with the notion of substitution because it fits best into their scheme. McIntyre points to the football match from which a player is removed to make way for a substitute who now plays instead of him, so that the removed player has no further part in the game. So Christ as our substitute pays the penalty for our sins instead of us, so that we do not have to pay it for ourselves.

Those who speak of Christ's action as vicarious want to avoid substitutionary language because of its penal associations but nevertheless want to do justice to the fact that on the cross Christ did for us what only he could do and that we could not do for ourselves.

More liberal approaches to the atonement prefer the language of representation, because it leaves open the responsibility of the people represented to make their own or to repudiate what has been done in their name. This goes well with an approach like that of Paul Fiddes' in which all the emphasis falls not on what Christ has done for us but on the response we make to it here and now. As McIntyre puts it:

> . . . the person who acts as substitute actually stands in the place that should be occupied by the one for whose sake the substitution is taking place. It is as if the substitute were that other person. The representative, on the contrary, keeps his own place, and the one he is representing keeps his, but the representative is empowered to act on behalf of the other person.[4]

McIntyre also interestingly correlates the three terms to the Greek prepositions used in the New Testament to describe Christ's work in relation to us: *anti*, 'instead of', suggests substitution but is used only occasionally; *hyper*, translated by 'on behalf of', goes with vicariousness, but translated 'in the interests of' suggests representation.[5]

Amidst such subtle distinctions how shall we find our way ahead? My own feeling is that the language of vicariousness is preferable to the other two if only because it carries less theological baggage and can therefore be more adequately moulded by the New Testament data that it is being used to express. Substitution language, apart from its associations with penal theories, is too excluding to do justice to our incorporation into Christ which a passage like Romans 6 describes and which both the gospel sacraments presuppose. Representation language on the other hand can easily be used to minimise our dependence on Christ and what he has done. A representative, for example a lawyer or a Member of Parliament, is usually appointed by those whom he represents and his authority to act depends on those who have appointed him. He can do only what they authorise and are prepared to ratify. By such a criterion Jesus is the representative not of us but of his Father. It is by the Father's authority that he does what he does and it is the Father who validates his atoning work by raising him from the dead.

To say that Christ's work on the cross is vicarious allows us to emphasise that, on the one hand, he does for us what we could not do for ourselves, and on the other that what he does, by its whole thrust and intention, is directed towards our subsequent involvement in it. The prepositional phrase 'on our behalf', translating as it does the New Testament *hyper*, infers both that something is being done by another because we could not do it ourselves, and also that it is done on our behalf and therefore we are involved in it and affected by it. The atoning work of Christ has both these aspects and we can look at them briefly in turn.

(a) What He did in our Place

So, what did Jesus on the cross do for us that we could not do for ourselves? That is the question that substitutionary theories of atonement want to press, and justice must be done to their concern even if not in their language. In the last two chapters, we have already indicated how we would answer and need only summarise here.

(i) He Responded for Us

As a man totally aligned with his Father's purpose and completely reflecting his Father's holiness, Jesus was able to offer to God in our humanity the response which his holy love required of our humanity. His was the sacrifice that was pure and without blemish that none could offer but he. What God had failed to find in the first Adam, he found in the last Adam.

(ii) He Repented for Us

Therefore, in identification with the sinful human situation in which all the rest of us were inextricably trapped and compromised, he achieved on our behalf a repentance, a *metanoia*, a turning back to God of our humanity which was possible only to someone who was pure enough to know what sin meant and what holiness meant and how the one could be overcome by the other. In so doing he made our humanity again acceptable to his Father.

(iii) He Bore Judgement for Us

As Son of God of one being with the Father, and therefore able to do what only God can do, he executed the divine judgement on sin and evil. He did this by exposing it in all its crucifying and death-dealing reality and overcoming it by the only thing that was greater than it: the outpouring in the midst of it of the holy divine love. Thus the divine justice is satisfied in the repudiation and rejection of evil and in the making right of what has been wrong, as Jesus turned our wrong into his right on the cross. In so doing he demonstrated and enacted his own and his Father's gracious and unconditional will to forgive.

(iv) He Remade Humanity for Us

As Son of God, of one being with the Father, and therefore able to do what only God can do, he recreated in himself a new humanity which is the first fruits of a new creation, the beginning and the promise of a new heaven and a new earth. In the reality of his crucified humanity, Jesus has plumbed the eschatological depths of sin, suffering and death and made common cause with both their victims and their perpetrators. In the reality of his risen humanity he is the promise of God's new life to the suffering, the sinful and the dead. What would have been a dead end for us becomes in him a new and living way to the Father and a grounded promise and substantiated hope that his gracious purposes for his whole creation will be fulfilled.

(v) He Fufilled the Covenant for Us

As Son of God, of one being with the Father and therefore able to do what only God can do, he can act on behalf of all humanity by himself becoming human and fulfilling the covenant that God had inaugurated from both sides. On the cross Jesus not only acts in his Father's name showing that he is our God, but as Creator and covenant Lord he has authority to act in our name and to fulfil the covenant on our behalf, so that in him and in his response to his Father we become again God's people.

Human beings can act for each other only in very limited ways

and the authority of a representative comes from those who are
represented. Only God as Creator and Lord is able to act vicariously in the name of his whole creation and has his authority to
do so in himself and not in us. Jesus does indeed act on our
behalf, but his appointment to do so comes not from his relationship to us but from his relationship to the Father. It is by God's
authority that he offers himself vicariously first for us and then to
us: 'This is my blood of the renewed covenant which is shed for
you and for many for the taking away of sin.'

R. C. Moberly comments:

> There is a perfectly unique possibility in the Son of God, of
> representing all mankind and dying as the representative
> of all; a possibility which, if it rests in one direction on the
> verity of his manhood, rests no less on his being the Logos
> who was with God and was God – the Life of life, the Image
> of the Father, the Creator of all created being; a possibility,
> therefore, which cannot even be conceived on any other side,
> or in any other person.[6]

In other words, if Christ is of one being with God, the possibilities
of what he can do for the rest of us far exceed the possibilities of
what one human creature can do for another. Those who deny
the divinity of Christ can have no proper understanding of his
vicarious action on our behalf, because they must needs limit it to
what one person can do for another. But if Jesus is one in being
with God, the only measure we can have of what the Creator can
do for his creatures when he becomes man is what he has actually
done when he came as man in Christ – namely died and risen
again for us all.

Thus the Christian claim embodied in the word and sacraments of the gospel and so in the worship and theology of the
Church, is that Jesus' vicarious action on behalf of all of us
depends on the uniqueness of both his humanity and his divinity.
In the double *homoöusios* of his oneness with us and his oneness
with the Father, he is able to do for us what none but he could do.
He brings into our situation what only one who came from God
could bring, and in the uniqueness of his divine–human action he
deals with the past in which the covenant has been broken and
opens the future in which it and all things are made new.

(b) Our Participation in Christ

We have looked at the side of his vicarious action in which he acts and from which we are excluded, but now we are to look at the other side in which we emphasise that his acting on our behalf was altogether with a view to our participation in what he has done. As T. F. Torrance puts it: 'Jesus Christ is our human response to God. Thus we appear before God and are accepted by him as those who are inseparably united to Jesus Christ our great High Priest in his eternal self-presentation to the Father.'[7] In this chapter, following the clues provided by the gospel sacraments, we have been describing that inseparable union as our incorporation into the body of the crucified and risen Lord whose action in the past defines his life and power in the present and so is available to us through his gospel and in his Spirit.

We have spoken of the renewal of our life by him. This is not so much in terms of the infusion of his life into ours as of the participation of our life into his. Paul speaks much more of our being in Christ than he does of Christ being in us. The second is of course an implication of the first and underlines the personal intimacy of the communion established, but the primary movement at this juncture is not from him to us but from us to him, although we cannot fully describe what is happening here without considering the action of the Holy Spirit, as we shall do later in the chapter.

There is however a way of talking of our relationship with him which suggests that what he has done on the cross remains in the realm of possibility and mere potentiality until it is made real and actual by our participation in it. This is yet another way of suggesting what we have been resisting throughout this book: that the decisive moment is the moment of our participation rather than the moment of Christ's action on our behalf. The new humanity needs no action or response of ours to move it out of the realm of possibility into the realm of actuality. It became real and actual at Calvary and it remains for ever real, actual and powerful at the right hand of the Father, whether we know of it or not, trust ourselves to it or not. The question is not how it can gain reality and actuality by being joined to us, but rather how we can attain ultimate reality and actuality by being joined to the risen and ascended Jesus whose humanity it is.

3. *A Trinitarian Analogy*

If we now go on to look more closely at the character of that incorporation and how it is effected and sustained, it will be helpful to adopt a Trinitarian analogy. The relationship between Christ and his people in the body of his Church mirrors the relationship of Father, Son and Holy Spirit within the life of God. That is why the Eastern tradition has often spoken of our incorporation into Christ as our divinisation, not at all meaning that we become God, but rather that as we are related through Christ and in the Spirit to the Father, the nature and character of the divine life with its relationships is reflected in ours.

The scriptural justification for such an approach is in the words of Jesus in the High Priestley prayer in John 17, where Jesus prays to his Father for his disciples that they 'may also be in us so that the world may believe that you have sent me. I have given them the glory that you gave me, that they may be one as we are one: I in them and you in me' (John 17:20–3). To be incorporated into the Son is to participate in the Son's relationship to the Father. The relationship of the disciples, primarily to Christ but subsequently to one another, is to be of the same nature as the relation of the Son to the Father.

We can examine the implications of this in several related points:

(a) Our Incorporation is Personal

Our incorporation into Christ is a union that, however close and intimate, always remains a union of persons whose distinctness from one another is retained and is indeed integral to it. Father, Son and Spirit are indeed *homoöusios* but that does not abolish the distinctions of persons between them and their unity remains a community of persons and is constituted by the relationship of persons. It is a union that is manifested in the Father's sending of his Son, in the Son's attentiveness and obedience to the Father, in the Spirit's work in glorifying both Father and Son. The Father never becomes the Son or the Spirit, the Spirit and the Son are never absorbed into the Father.

So with our incorporation into Christ we share his life in its new humanity, which is reconciled to the Father, and we become the body of which he is the head, but there is no mystical absorption of us into him. In Galatians 2:20 Paul emphasises the closeness of the union and our total dependence on what Christ has done for us by saying: 'I no longer live but Christ lives in me.' However he immediately explains that sharing of life in I–Thou personalist language: 'The life I life in the body, I live by faith in the Son of God who loved me and gave himself for me.' It is a real and vital union but it remains a union of trust in one person for another. That is why the union between God and his people in the Old Testament and between Christ and his Church in the New is often compared to the union of husband and wife where the two partners become 'one flesh' but the oneness is constituted by the personal relation of the two persons to each other (c.f. Eph. 5:31–2).

(b) Incorporation is Self-giving

Our incorporation into Christ is a union that is constituted by the self-giving of the two parties to each other. Here also the Trinitarian analogy holds. The unity of the Godhead is the Father's giving himself to the Son in the Spirit and the Son's responsive giving of himself in the same Spirit to the Father. So our incorporation into Christ consists of his giving of himself in the Spirit to us – 'The Son of God who loved me and gave himself for me' – and our responsive giving of ourselves in the same Spirit to him – 'the life I live in the body, I live by faith in the Son of God.'

Christ's self-giving to us is his grace, our responsive self-giving of ourselves to him is the faith that he inspires in us, and it is by grace through faith that we are delivered from our sinful past and liberated for our Christ-centred future. The locus, the meeting point of his grace and our faith, is our sin and our suffering, our godlessness and our god-forsakenness. He comes to us in that place, as he first came to it on Calvary, with all the resources of his incarnate deity to convert the place that is without and against God to the place that is with God and open to God. He comes to convert our old humanity that is under sentence of death into a new humanity that is in living relationship with the Father. We are drawn to the place where his grace awaits us in a faith that knows that we cannot live out of ourselves – 'It is no longer I that live' – but have to live out of what another brings to us.

That is what faith is, the trusting of yourself either partially or totally to another and what that other can do for you. Faith in Christ is faith at its most radical because it is a trusting of ourselves to another out of a total mistrust of ourselves when we are left to ourselves. That is why Paul sees trust in our ability to fulfil the requirements of God's law as the antithesis of faith, because it is the religious manifestation of a proud self-confidence. Faith in Christ, on its positive side, is a trust of ourselves totally to another in the things that matter most to us, our freedom, our future, the whole nature and character of our relationships with God and with other people. These things are beyond all our attaining and striving; they have to be received with empty hands stretched out to the crucified and risen Lord.

Our incorporating union with Christ does indeed consist of a mutual self-giving of persons, of him to us and of us to him, but what each brings to that union is of course entirely diverse and different. He comes to it from Calvary with, in the words of the *Book of Common Prayer*, 'all the benefits of his passion'; we come to it, seeing at least something of our need, for what only he can give. His is the self-giving of his accepted sacrifice and his new humanity; ours is the receptive self-giving of those who are at least partially aware of their total dependence on him, of how dead they are without him and who therefore look to him as the only source of the renewal of life they require.

That is the self-giving of faith that is integral to our incorporation into Christ, not just at the beginning in the initiating incorporation of our baptism, but all the way through. The nearer I get to Christ, the longer I live with him, the more conscious shall I become of my continuing plight without him and my need for him, the more in faith I will cling to his cross. Again and again we have to come to the Eucharist with empty hands to receive of the fullness of his body and blood, of his new humanity which he brings to us from the cross. And, as Donald Baillie reminds us,[8] the self-giving of faith and the receptivity of faith are in this context the same thing. We receive Christ's provision for our need in our giving of ourselves in all our neediness to him.

(c) Incorporation is into his Death and Risen Life

Because our incorporation into Christ involves this mutual and dynamic self-giving, our insertion into his life results in the manifestation of the signs of his life in us. Furthermore the pattern of his life as it moves from death into life is also the continuing pattern of our lives in him. This is the whole point of what Paul has to say about our baptism in Romans 6: 'We were therefore buried with him through baptism into death in order that, just as Christ was raised from the dead through the glory of the Father, we too may live a new life' (Rom. 6:4).

We are baptised into both his death and his resurrection; the Christian life consists of a double process of death and resurrection, and we are to view our lives in these terms: 'In the same way, count yourselves dead to sin but alive to God in Christ Jesus' (Rom. 6:11). The result of our incorporation into Christ is a continual dying to sin, a developing and increasing unresponsiveness to all the things that have alienated us from God and from his purposes for us. This leads on to a continual coming alive to God, a developing and increasing attentiveness to God and our own assent to and involvement in his purposes for us. Jesus in John makes the same point in terms of seeds and harvests: 'I tell you the truth, unless a grain of wheat falls to the ground and dies, it remains only a single seed. But if it dies, it produces many seeds. The man who loves his life will lose it, while the man who hates his life in this world will keep it for eternal life' (John 12:24–5). Here again the dying and the harvesting are seen as Christ's own way from Calvary to Easter and therefore as the way through denial of self to renewal of life for his people.

To return to Romans 6, it is important to note that in this passage our identification with Christ in his death is treated as present fact, and our participation in his resurrection to new humanity is still future: 'If we have been united with him like this in his death, we will certainly also be united with him in his resurrection. For we know that our old self was crucified with him so that the body of sin might be done away with, that we should no longer be slaves to sin' (Rom. 6:5–6). In the midst of his well-grounded assurance that the resurrection of Jesus means our resurrection, because we have been baptised into him, Paul maintains a sober, realistic eschatology according to which our present agenda is preoccupied chiefly with our liberation from our alienation and the full and final manifestation of the new humanity which is still to come. Any hyper-enthusiastic version of the Christian life that wants to get on to the revival of life without the struggle and agony of the dying to sin will end up in delusion and self-deception. There is no way to the coming alive in Christ that does not require personal, practical and costly participation in his death to sin. For him that dying is once for all in the eschatological finality of his passion and rising, for us the dying is protracted in our living and only at our death is it complete.

(d) Incorporation is into a Community

Our incorporation into Christ involves our incorporation into the community of which Christ is head. In the Trinitarian life of God the three persons are who they are and do what they do only in their relationships to one another. Therefore to be incorporated into Christ means that we are who we are and we do what we do only in relationship to everyone else who is in relationship to him. Our incorporation is always personal but never individualistic. In both baptism and Eucharist we are dealt with one by one, but never in isolation. Because our baptism is into Christ, it is also into the community that belongs to Christ and its promise of new life can be nurtured and fulfilled only within that community. Similarly, as Paul makes clear to the Corinthians, to eat the bread and wine of the Lord's Supper and to fail to relate to those who share it with us is to court condemnation: 'For anyone who eats and drinks without recognising the body of the Lord eats and drinks judgement on himself. That is why many among you are weak and sick, and a number of you have fallen asleep' (1 Cor. 11:29–30).

This means that the pattern of cross and resurrection, of dying and rising, operates not only in the lives of individuals but in the corporate history and experience of the Church, both universally and locally. As the Church moves towards its *eschaton* it has to go through periods of dying and declining, when, in the providence of God, there is exposure and rejection of the things that at that time most alienate it from its participation in God's mission to the world, whether because they are in contradiction to that mission or have become irrelevant to it. There are also periods when a Church that is near to death and has become like the valley of dry bones of which Ezekiel speaks,[9] is brought back to a new hearing of God's life-giving word and a new openness to God's life-giving Spirit and in faithfulness to that gospel comes alive in a new way. At the centre of that revivification there will be a new and relevant relationship in confession, in repentance (*metanoia*) and in intercession to the crucified and risen Christ.

One could indeed write a history of the Church, and indeed a history of every local congregation, in terms of its incorporation into the death and rising of Jesus. A Church that belongs to Christ will not escape either and indeed both will always be at work, although at different periods one will be more evident than the other. In the deadest days signs of resurrection will not be entirely lacking, in the times of renewal there will be much that still needs to die. The Lord of the Church has sounded the depths of death and climbed the heights of glory and is with his people both in their dying and their living. To follow him means to keep on becoming involved in this dynamic process of costly dying and rejuvenated rising from the dead.

(e) Incorporation is the Work of the Spirit

Our incorporation into Christ is Trinitarian because it is the work of the Holy Spirit. There is an essential relationship between the death of Christ on Calvary and the outpouring of the Holy Spirit at Pentecost which is not primarily about sensational experiences of tongues and prophecies but about our incorporation into the crucified and risen Lord. Moberly puts it like this:

> . . . Calvary is the condition, precedent and enabling to Pentecost. The objective reality is completed first that it may be indeed subjectively realised. Christ is crucified first and risen before our eyes; that Christ crucified and risen may be the secret love and power of our hearts. Calvary without Pentecost would not be an atonement to us. But Pentecost would not be without Calvary, Calvary is the possibility of Pentecost: and Pentecost is the realisation in human spirits, of Calvary.[10]

The Johannine scheme makes the connection even closer, as we have seen with the breathing of the Spirit upon the disciples by the resurrected Lord who has just shown them his hands and his side and is incorporating them in the ongoing mission with which the Father has entrusted him (John 20:19–23).

The Spirit who, as we have suggested, was already present and active on Calvary, holding Christ in relationship with his Father even in the midst of his abandoned desolation, reaches out to others as the Spirit of the crucified and risen Lord to incorporate others into his dying and his living. That is the thought behind 1 Corinthians 15:45: 'The last Adam [became] life-giving Spirit.' The new humanity that has passed through death to life is so filled with the Spirit that it reaches out to draw into itself those on whose behalf it has suffered and triumphed. The Christ who is lifted up to die, to love, to reign draws all people to himself (John 12), and this he does by his Spirit.

It is the Spirit who makes our relationship with Christ which is historically mediated ('This do in remembrance of me') into an immediate relationship with the ascended Lord ('Take eat, this is my body'). It is the Spirit who bridges the spiritual distance between the High Priest who is with the Father in the mystery of his glory and his people still here on earth. It is the Spirit who convinces the world of sin and righteousness and judgement and gives us that insight into what Christ has done for us. It is the Spirit by whom we are born again into a new relationship with the Father and the Son. It is the Spirit who creates the dynamic unity between the person of Christ and the human persons who by faith are made one with him.

This means that our incorporation into Christ is not an achievement of ours to be set alongside his atoning work for us. The faith that turns to him is not something that has its source in us, our contribution to our own salvation, without which what he has done would be insufficient and in vain, like an offer that was made but not accepted. His work, which was done for us and in the Spirit, reaches out by the same Spirit and through the word and sacraments of the gospel involves us in it. 'Because of his great love for us, God, who is rich in mercy, made us alive with Christ even when we were dead in transgressions – it is by grace you have been saved' (Eph. 2:4–5). Our coming alive with Christ is itself the work of God in us, as is the faith by which we receive that new life: 'For it is by grace you have been saved, through faith – and this not from yourselves, it is the gift of God' (Eph. 2:8). Our reaching out to him in our faith is itself the result of his reaching into us by his Spirit, it is a communication of his humanity that has died and come to life by its faith in the Father.

(f) Incorporation is our Free Act

At the same time the Holy Spirit who acts in us is the Spirit of freedom: 'Where the Spirit of the Lord is, there is freedom' (2 Cor. 3:17). The Spirit communicates to us the freedom of the new man, Jesus, to relate to God and to his purposes. Pannenberg, with specific reference to Karl Barth, rightly warns against such an over-emphasis on the objective validity of the atoning work of Christ as would result in a kind of imposed reconciliation, a dictated salvation that sweeps us up into itself whether we know it or not, believe it or not, like it or not. In other words Christ has acted for us with such overwhelming sovereignty on our behalf that we are disqualified from any say in our own destiny and willy-nilly are made right with God. Pannenberg wonders 'whether the final result is not the total disappearance of our independent humanity'.[11]

Such an approach to the matter would be quite untrue to the New Testament with its insistence on the personal act of faith as the means by which we are able to participate in what Christ has done for us and thus to take responsibility for our acceptance of it and our identification with it – a process of reception with which, in my view, Barth never fully came to terms.

Our identification with Christ is our own act which each of us must do in freedom and for ourselves, for how could we participate in the free obedience of Christ except in freedom? But that freedom to act for ourselves is itself the gift of Christ by his Spirit; without it we remain slaves to our own alienation from God, from others and from ourselves. The freedom in which we are incorporated into Christ is itself the gift of Christ which he has won for us on the cross and communicates to us by his Spirit. It is the mark of the Spirit that what we could not do by ourselves, he enables us to do for ourselves. He takes the freedom for God, for others and for the world in which Christ lived, died and rose, and brings it to our side of the relationship, so that we are free to belong to him. That is the gift of free responsiveness that is

Christ's before it is ours but which becomes ours by his Spirit. As that Spirit incorporates us into that Christ we too begin to die to sin and come alive to God.

9

One Cross – For the Whole World

We have just been looking at the significance and power of the cross within the community that is integrated by its initial baptism and ongoing communion into the dying and the rising of Jesus. Now, however, we are to look beyond the believing Church and ask what Christ's work of atonement means for the rest of humanity that has not yet believed and may not even have heard the gospel. We are, in other words, concerned not just with the 'Once' but the 'For All' of our title. The 'Once' defines what we have called the unique distinctiveness of what was done on Calvary; the 'For All' indicates that what was done once is universally relevant to the whole of humanity in all other places and at all other times. The title itself of course is a piece of word play, but we have to look now at the biblical evidence for the universal claim that it embodies and try to see what that claim involves.

To deal with such an agenda adequately would take another book, since it would plunge us, for example, into all the complications and ambiguities of the inter-faith debate with all the questions about comparative religion and Christian uniqueness that it raises. Our aim here however has to be much more restricted and properly theological. Given the position about the meaning of the cross that I have been expounding and defending, what as Christians, whose whole trust and hope is in Christ crucified, are we to say about and hope for the vast majority of humanity who have not shared that trust?

In answering that question we are entering territory where guidance is scarce and conclusions have to be tentative, not least because the final outcome of the deed done in Calvary belongs to the ultimate future that is still hidden deep in the mystery of the Triune God, and we do well not to intrude too far on what is far beyond our ken. Nevertheless the Lord of the future and the eschatological Judge has become incarnate among us and what he has done for us in the past and goes on doing by his Spirit in the present offers valid if partial insights into what he will do finally in the future

1. Christ Died for All – The Biblical Evidence

There is quite overwhelming New Testament evidence that the scope of God's atoning action in Christ is the whole world. Once again the words spoken at the Last Supper give us reliable access into the mind of Jesus when, over the cup, he speaks of the blood of the new covenant 'poured out for many' (Mark 14:24, c.f. Matt. 26:28). On this usage, Joachim Jeremias has, with general scholarly acceptance, pointed out:

> Whereas 'many' in Greek (as in English) is in opposition to 'all', and so has an exclusive connotation ('many but not all') the Hebrew can have an inclusive connotation ('the whole, comprising many individuals'). This linguistic usage comes about because Hebrew and Aramaic have no word for 'all' in the plural.[1]

C. E. B. Cranfield quotes even Calvin to the same effect: 'By the word *many*, he means not a part of the world only, but the whole human race.'[2]

That the intention of Jesus was understood in this inclusive and universal sense is made clear by the other main New Testament witnesses. In John the incarnation and atonement are set from the start in a cosmic setting. The one who became incarnate as Jesus of Nazareth is the Word by whom the world was made, he is hailed from the start as 'the Lamb of God who takes away the sin of the world' (John 1:29). He is sent into the world so that the world through him might be saved (3:17) and he goes to his death proclaiming that this hour anticipates the last judgement when all things are put to rights, and, through his being lifted up to die, he will draw all people to himself (16:31–2).

Equally in the Pauline writings the work of atonement is seen in the same universal and inclusive context: 'God was reconciling the world to himself in Christ' (2 Cor. 5:19) and on that basis we can summon all people to be reconciled to God (5:18–21).

Furthermore, as we have seen, Jesus crucified and risen is, in Romans and 1 Corinthians, presented as the second and the ultimate Adam. It is indeed from Jewish stock that he springs, as the son of David and the seed of Abraham, but he is also the antitype of Adam, who is the prototype of sin-alienated humanity. Therefore his relevance and the extent of his mission is to humanity as such.

The specific Jewish experience exposes the universal human predicament. It is to the sin and suffering at the heart of that universal predicament that Jesus addresses himself on the cross, where there is no racial distinction between Jew and Gentile, gender distinction between man and woman, social distinction between the bound and the free. He meets us all at the lowest common denominator where we are all assailed by our suffering and in the process of being destroyed by our sin. The Messiah of Israel is also the Saviour of the world.

So, in his account of salvation history in Romans 9–11, Paul describes a period in which the divine saving action was concentrated on Israel with a view to the ultimate inclusion of the Gentile world, followed by another period in which it was concentrated on the mainly Gentile church for the sake of the ultimate reintegration of Israel. Both these phases are temporary, however prolonged, and are seen as stages on the journey to a final fulfilment when the fullness of the Gentiles are gathered in and all Israel will be saved (Rom. 11:25–6). Paul, speaking about the Jews to the Gentiles at Rome, sums up his conclusions: 'Just as you who were at one time disobedient to God have now received mercy as a result of their disobedience, so they too have now become disobedient in order that they too may now receive mercy as a result of God's mercy to you. *For God has bound all men over to disobedience so that he may have mercy on them all*' (Rom. 11:30–2). The refusals of grace, the rebellions against God that in all sorts of different forms mark and mar human history in both its communal and its personal expressions, are not final. The Christian hope is that the disobedience that causes such pain and havoc will in the end yield to the mercy that restores right relationships with God and among people. That mercy has its focus on Calvary and exercises its renewing power from the cross.

The cosmic optimism that has its source in Calvary has its most explicit expression in the final development of the Pauline corpus

in Ephesians and Colossians, whether from Paul's own hand or
that of a disciple. So, as we have already reminded ourselves, he
speaks in Ephesians of how: 'In him [Christ] we have redemption
through his blood, the forgiveness of sins, in accordance with the
riches of God's grace that he lavished on us with all wisdom and
understanding. And he made known to us the mystery of his will
according to his good pleasure, which he purposed in Christ, to
be put into effect when the times will have reached their fulfilment – *to bring all things in heaven and on earth together under one
head, even Christ*' (Eph. 1:7–10). The present experience of God's
redeeming grace in the Church gives insight into and confidence
about God's ultimate purpose for the whole universe. What he
has already done for us and has begun to work out in us, he has
also done for the whole created universe and the day will come
when he will fulfil that purpose on that cosmic scale. Colossians
bears witness to the same purpose in the same relationship to the
experienced power of the cross: 'For God was pleased to have all
his fullness dwell in him, and through him to reconcile to himself
all things, whether things on earth or things in heaven, by
making peace through his blood, shed on the cross' (Col. 1:19–20).

It is clear from both these passage that the work of the cross
extends beyond humanity to the whole of creation. Everything
that was made through Christ is also to be redeemed through
Christ. That can happen because the demonic forces, the princi-
palities and powers that have interfered with God's purpose for
his creation, have been overthrown at the cross.

The same context is hinted at in the mysterious verses of
Romans 8 in which Paul suggests that the renewal of creation is
dependent upon the reconciliation of humanity back into its filial
relationship with God: 'The creation waits in eager expectation
for the sons of God to be revealed. For the creation was subjected
to frustration, not by its own choice, but by the will of the one
who subjected it, in hope that the creation itself will be liberated
from its bondage to decay and brought into the glorious freedom
of the children of God' (Rom. 8:19–21). In Genesis 3, when the
man and the woman fell out with God, the whole creation fell out
of God's purpose for it. But now, in the new Adam, humanity is
put right with God and the liberation of creation from frustration
will follow when that new humanity comes into its own. Such an
insight, making, as it does, the renewal of creation depend on the
renewal of humanity which itself is dependent on the atoning

work of Christ, has all sorts of important ecological implications
which we cannot pursue here.

From all these New Testament sources we can see how unani-
mously the death of Jesus was seen in these quite universal terms.
God's purpose in the living, dying and rising of his Son was
directed to the whole of humanity and through it to the whole of
the created world. This is the basis of the Church's mission. The
crucified and risen Christ has been given 'all authority in heaven
and on earth' and his people are sent out 'into all the world to
make disciples of all the nations' (Matt. 28:18–19). Where the
Church loses its confidence in the cross, it loses its confidence in
its mission. Unless the atoning work of Christ is at the centre of its
message, the Church's gospel loses its distinctiveness, its cutting
edge and its healing power.

2. The Double Outcome of the Gospel

But the work of Christ which is relevant to all humanity because
it is at its heart a renewal of humanity, is in fact received only by
some people. In the mission of the Church, there is a double
outcome. Some, in fact the vast majority of those who have lived
in the last two thousand years, do not hear at all and so cannot
believe and, among those who are addressed, some respond with
faith and others turn away in unbelief, indifference and even
outright hostility. As Bishop Gavin Reid once put it, expounding
the parable of the sower, the word that any evangelist will hear
more often than any other is the word No. The atoning act is done
'for many'; it is received by few.

That leaves us with two questions. The first has a long history
in the Church. How can we relate the incomplete response to the
preaching of the cross to the will of God that acts savingly for all
of us on the cross? Jesus said he would draw all people to himself,
but all the evidence down the centuries is that in fact he has
drawn only some. The second question is even more perplexing.
What is the relationship of the atoning work of Christ to those
who have never heard of it or who look to quite different cultural
and religious traditions for the things that it offers them? That is a
modern question much discussed in a pluralist world where the
segregation of cultures and religions has been broken down and

Christians are increasingly aware that theirs is far from being the only answer to the human predicament. At the end of a book in which we have been contending for the unique distinctiveness of the cross of Jesus as God's remedy for our predicament, what shall we say? We shall discuss these two questions in turn.

(a) Double Predestination and Limited Atonement

One way of coping with the double outcome of the preaching of the gospel is to accept the finality of the situation as it stands and allow it to restrict and condition the universal biblical statements that we have just been outlining. Jesus died for all but his death will benefit only some. There are two ways of understanding this constriction; one ascribes it to the divine will, the other to the human. *Arminianism*   *predestination*

The first of these is the hyper-Calvinist approach, which absolutises the double outcome of the gospel by driving it back into the eternal purpose and will of God himself. This speaks of double predestination and limited atonement. From eternity to eternity God chose some whom he willed to save from the consequences of their sin by the death of his Son and thus manifested his undeserved and gracious love towards them. The rest he left unchosen to face the deadly consequences that his justice meted out to their sins. Christ died therefore, not for all people, but only for those whom God had chosen and who therefore by the Holy Spirit would be brought to justifying and sanctifying faith when they heard the gospel.

Such an approach cannot be reconciled with the universal implications of the biblical passages that we have cited above. The usual strategy is to suggest that the biblical 'all people' means 'all sorts of people' rather than 'everyone'. The elect would include, for example, some Jews, some Gentiles, some men, some women, some wise, some foolish and so on. So Jesus is seen as promising to draw some people from every category to himself, but of course, by implication, not to draw others.

That points to the other great difficulty with which the proponents of this view have always struggled. How in preaching can we call everybody to become incorporated into the new humanity defined by Christ's death and rising while at the same time we know that some of our hearers are by the very decree of

God himself prevented from responding to that call? It can easily seem that God is offering Christ with his open gospel hand and simultaneously taking him way with his closed predestinating hand, and that is not an attitude consonant with the revealed character of the God and Father of our Lord Jesus Christ.

This is indeed the main point against this whole approach made by John McLeod Campbell, whose whole career was a long and costly struggle against double predestination and limited atonement, because he saw it as theologically destructive of the heart of the gospel and pastorally disastrous in the life of the Scottish Church of his day.

Double predestination and limited atonement will not do basically because it misrepresents the nature and character of God revealed in Christ. Responding to John Owen and Jonathan Edwards, the typical representatives of the view he was criticising, Campbell says:

> While they set forth justice as a necessary attribute of the divine nature, so that God must deal with *all* men according to its requirements, they represent mercy and love as not necessary, but arbitrary, and what therefore may find their expression in the history of *only some* men. For according to their system justice alone is expressed in the history of all men, that is to say, in the history of the non-elect, in their endurance of punishment; in the history of the elect, in Christ's enduring it for them. Mercy and love are expressed in the history of the elect alone.[3]

He then goes on to draw out the pastoral implications of this theological position: 'But is it fair to ask men to put their trust in that God of whom we cannot tell them whether He loves them or does not? In that Saviour of whom we cannot tell them whether He died for them or did not?'[4]

The flaw at the heart of this view is the doubt it casts on the ultimacy of the love of God in his attitude to his people and his creation. Fundamentally he is a God of Justice who gives sinners what they deserve and his love and mercy are restricted to those he has, for inscrutable reasons of his own, decided to redeem. The accepting love of Jesus for people cannot be trusted as an ultimate expression of the Father's character and nature, since there are those whom he has decided not to accept and not to love.

'Those who have seen me may or may not have seen the Father.' His love, far from being unconditional grace, is conditioned and restricted by his decree. I do not know whether it applies to me and I am therefore condemned to an anxious and endless introspection as to whether or not I can discern in myself credible signs of election. The gloomy uncertainty of that search haunted Scottish religion year upon year, until such as McLeod Campbell taught again the ultimacy of the love of the Father which was revealed in the atoning work of the Son and could be trusted because its grace extended to all.

Such a rediscovery was at the heart of the Wesleyan revival and the joyful assurance of it runs through its praise:

Father, whose everlasting love, thine only Son for sinners gave,
Whose grace to all did freely move, and sent him down the
  world to save.
Thy undistinguishing regard was cast on Adam's fallen race,
For all thou hast in Christ prepared, sufficient, sovereign saving
  grace.
The world he suffered to redeem. For all he has the atonement
  made;
for those who will not come to him the ransom of his life was
  paid.

A polemical hymn indeed, but who ever sang with such assurance and joy over limited atonement?

In the course of God's history with his people there are choosings and rejectings: the election of Israel from among the nations, the choice of Jacob rather than Esau to be the bearer of the divine purpose. Nevertheless these double outcomes are never ultimate, they are never the final expression of God's will but rather stages on the road to the revelation in Christ of God's love for the whole world and the giving of his Son that the whole world might be saved.

(b) The Arminian Alternative

There is however another way of treating the double outcome of the proclamation of the gospel as ultimate and final, and this will have a far greater appeal to Christians shaped by our culture than double predestination or limited atonement. On this view the ultimate factor in the reception of the gospel is not the predestinating divine will but the deciding human will. This is the Arminian or semi-Pelagian approach that has dominated so much American-based evangelism in the last century, but also has deep roots in Catholic tradition and an inveterate attraction for many English, although not so many Scottish, Christians. This view makes much of the unfettered freedom of the human will in our responding to the gospel. Each of us must make our own decision to accept or reject what Christ offers to us. God will treat us not as puppets but as people, will respect and never force our decision and it will be on that decision that our eternal relationship to God in Christ will, for good or ill, for salvation or damnation, ultimately depend. The message is that God has done his wonderful best for us in Christ, and now it all depends on us ourselves whether his dying and rising love will have its way with us or be refused and frustrated. The last word is not with him but with us and, by the consequences of what we decide both he and we must for ever abide. Such a view is both flattering and fearsome, flattering because it tells us that in the last resort we are the disposers of our own destiny, and fearsome because it places the whole responsibility for that back in our own hands. Christ makes our salvation possible, but we ourselves must make it actual.

From a New Testament perspective there are however many questions to be asked of such an approach. Do we not flatter ourselves more than a little when we see ourselves as independent free agents competent to stand in our freedom over against the gospel and reach our own individual decisions about it? Is our human condition not more realistically described by Paul when he says that, left to ourselves, we are 'slaves to sin' with sinful minds that are hostile to God (Rom. 8:5) so that our alienation from God prevents us from knowing him and from being able to respond positively to him? Our freedom to be in right relationship with God is the very thing that we have lost and that needs to be restored to us before we are in any position to decide anything.

Our ability to respond to Christ does not have its source in ourselves, but is itself his gift to us. The faith that relates us to him is not something that we can lay on or summon up by an act of will, it is created in us by our exposure to Jesus and his gospel. To

[margin note: like Calvin's critique makes us God's]

quote Ephesians again: 'For it is by grace you have been saved, through faith – and this not from yourselves, it is the gift of God' (Eph. 2:8). The whole package, not just the grace that gives itself for us but the faith that that grace creates in us and elicits from us – the whole package from beginning to end – is the gift of God.

To say the same thing another way, the Arminian pattern of the autonomous individual deciding about and disposing of Christ and his gospel has little room for the Holy Spirit. The Holy Spirit in the New Testament is the Spirit of responsiveness who first comes from the Father to the Son to enable him in his responsiveness and who then is given to us by the Son to enable our responsiveness to him and his atoning and renewing work. That responding faith and repentance must indeed become authentically our own, the genuine expression of the new heart and will that have been created in us. A response that is personal to each of us is indeed an indispensable factor in our incorporation into Christ and the Arminian understanding does well to emphasise that fact. But that responsiveness, although it is indeed ours, does not have its origin in us, but rather in God the Holy Spirit.

So to confess the Lordship of Jesus is the gift of the Spirit (1 Cor. 12:3); if we relate to God as Father it is because the Spirit of Jesus is crying *Abba* in our inmost hearts (Gal. 4:6). If we are able to pray, it is because the Spirit of prayer has been given to us (Rom. 8:26). If we are beginning to be changed into Christ's likeness from one degree of glory to another, this comes from the Spirit (2 Cor. 3.18). If we have gifts for ministry, these are elicited by the Spirit (1 Cor. 12). Scientists nowadays talk much of energy fields; the Holy Spirit is an energy field of responsiveness and to be born again of the Spirit is to be drawn into that field and begin to make his responsiveness our own. All our responsiveness to God, the Father and the Son comes to us from the Spirit who is the Spirit of the Father and the Son. It is he who starts it all by choosing us, and only then can we choose him (John 15:16).

(c) The Universal Hope

The double outcome of the gospel in history shows that the Holy Spirit as well as the Son can be despised and rejected, the Holy Spirit of responsiveness knows what it is like to have to yield to the unholy spirit of human autonomy and rebelliousness.

Paul exhorts his friends in Ephesus: 'Do not grieve the Holy Spirit of God, with whom you were sealed for the day of redemption' (Eph. 4:30). May we not say that in this alienated world the Holy Spirit is often grieved, just as Jesus was once crucified, not only by Christians in their frequent lapses into disobedience, but fundamentally by those who, in the bonds of their slavery to sin, resist the freedom to respond that he can give. The gospel is answered with the No of alienation rather than with the Yes of liberation.

But just as the triumph of evil is not the ultimate outcome of Calvary, so it cannot be the final outcome of the Spirit's mysterious encounter with the human heart. The Church from the first has looked in hope beyond the rejection of its Messiah by Jews and its Lord by Gentiles to the day when 'at the name of Jesus every knee should bow, in heaven and on earth and under the earth, and every tongue confess that Jesus Christ is Lord, to the glory of God the Father' (Phil. 2:10–11).

From the day when Saul of Tarsus walked the road to Damascus until now, the history of the Church is shot through by moments in which the crucified and risen Lord has triumphed in his Spirit by turning his most obdurate enemies into his most faithful friends. Church history is the story of a community that has often known black nights in which it has sold itself into captivity to powers of darkness and death that have enslaved it and thrown doubt on the validity of its gospel. But, in the mercy of God, these dark nights have been followed by wonderful mornings of resurrection when the Spirit of responsiveness has reasserted himself and opened what seemed a closed community to a new sharing in the life of Jesus.

In the same way, on a personal level, we have all known with Paul long periods in which the only thing that we could say about ourselves was: 'When I want to do good, evil is right there with me. For in my inner being I delight in God's law; but I see another law at work in the members of my body, waging war against the law of my mind and making me a prisoner of the law of sin at work within my members. What a wretched man I am! Who will rescue me from this body of death?' (Rom. 7:21–4). But we are not left there 'because through Christ Jesus the law of the Spirit of life set me free from the law of sin and death' (Rom. 8:2). The Spirit who is grieved and rejected shows himself again and

again to be the Lord and giver of life to the very people who have
turned him away.

Such moments of intervening and rescuing grace can be seen as
the earnests and first instalments of that incorporation into the
death and resurrection of Jesus which the Father purposes and
the Spirit enables for the whole creation. What the Spirit has
already done for some he seeks to do for all, because it was for all
that the Father sent his Son and it was for all that the Son offered
himself on the cross. Such a universal hope has, as we have tried
to show, good grounding in the New Testament scriptures. The
God who does not reject anyone, and does not abandon us to our
own choices, has in his Son and his Spirit the love that is mighty
enough to bring us all home to himself. All shall be well and all
manner of things shall be well, but only because Jesus has died
for the world and risen again.

If such statements look like an affirmation of universalism – the
doctrine that none will be lost and all will be saved – I would
want to insist that it is a very particular brand of universalism
that has to be carefully distinguished from other very different
teaching that often passes by that name.

(i) A Christocentric Universalism

It has to be distinguished from a pluralistic universalism that
teaches that God loves everybody so much that, quite apart from
what they believed and how they have lived, he will ultimately
accept them into right relationship with himself regardless. Such
teaching totally contradicts the whole position we have been
expounding in this book and would indeed render the atoning
work of the cross redundant and unnecessary.

For Christians the one living way back to the Father is by his
Son, Jesus Christ (John 14:5) and by being incorporated into
his dying and rising. The only universal salvation that is available
is that by his Spirit he should draw all people to himself. Pluralistic universalism bypasses the cross, but this kind of
Christocentric universalism exalts the cross as 'the full perfect
and sufficient, oblation and satisfaction for the sins of the whole
world.'[5] The only universal reconciliation is by a universal conversion (*metanoia*) to Christ and his gospel brought about in the
freedom that is the undeserved gift of the Spirit.

(ii) Universal Hope – not Dogma

This kind of universalism must remain in the realm of well-grounded hope rather than the realm of settled doctrine. The outcome of the evangelistic situation, in which the Holy Spirit encounters alienated human hearts, remains open rather than closed. There can indeed be a double outcome, either a defiant or unbelieving No or a believing and accepting Yes, not just at the beginning of the Christian life but all the way through.

Christians know both the grief of continuing enslavement to evil and the glory of a God-given ability to escape from its hold upon us. It belongs to the freedom of the Spirit who, like the wind, blows where he wills, to advance and to retire, to wait and to win and no one can tell what he will do in any given situation. And yet, though we cannot predict the tactics of the evangelistic battle, we do know that the strategy is for the ultimate drawing of all people to the lifted up Lord, and therefore, as we encounter the tribulations of the gospel in the world, we may have good hope in the Lord who has overcome the world.

(iii) The Warnings of Jesus

The openness and indeed the urgency of the evangelistic encounter is further emphasised by the repeated warnings of Jesus himself, summed up when he said: 'Enter through the narrow gate. For wide is the gate and broad is the road that leads to destruction, and many are entering through it. But small is the gate and narrow the road that leads to life, and only a few are finding it' (Matt. 7:13–14). Roads that lead away from God are roads that lead nowhere and, in the Israel of his day, as in our own world, many are walking on such roads and, if they persist in them, they will lead to their final undoing. Hell – final and fixed alienation from and rejection of the saving love of God – remains what Barth used to call an impossible possibility, even if the Christian hope is that hell may in the end prove to be empty.

Any optimistic universalism that ignores the fatal threat inherent in the sinful human situation shows itself to be merely facile and idealistic. The threat was so real that nothing but the death of the Son could cope with it. But, precisely because of his death, the hope remains that Jesus, who has himself walked on the road to destruction to its dire destination and descended

warnings of Jesus are real

into hell, has the power to overcome that threat and, in his Spirit
who flows from his cross, the ability to turn people back from it to
himself and the reconciliation with God he has achieved.

   In this situation, where nothing is fixed, everything may yet be
hoped for. The great question is whether we trust the Spirit of the
Christ who overcame the resistance and hostility that crucified
him to go on overcoming the same resistance and hostility that he
encounters still in human hearts and indeed in our own. It is
certainly true that there are strongholds of evil around us and
within us that still refuse to yield, but the question is whether we
put our confidence in them to maintain their resistance or in the
Spirit of Jesus to overcome it?

   I once heard Karl Barth say: 'I do not believe in universalism or
any other "ism", but I do believe in Jesus Christ, the Saviour of
the world and of all men.' Barth explains more formally why he
refuses to affirm a *doctrine* of universal salvation while at the
same time he maintains equally strongly a *hope* of universal salvation as follows:

> If we are certainly forbidden to count on this [universal res-
> toration] as though we had a claim to it, as though it were
> not supremely the work of God to which many can have no
> possible claim, we are surely commanded the more defi-
> nitely to hope and pray for it ... to hope and to pray
> cautiously and yet distinctly that, in spite of everything
> which may seem quite conclusively to proclaim the opposite,
> his compassion should not fail, and that in accordance with
> his mercy which is 'new every morning' he 'will not cast off
> for ever' (Lam. 33:22, 31).[6]

This is the prayer that according to Timothy is 'good and pleases
God our Saviour who wants all people to be saved and to come to
a knowledge of the truth. For there is one God and one mediator
between God and humankind, the man Christ Jesus, who gave
himself as a ransom for all.' The intercession arises from Christ's
mediation and so has good hope of an answer.

3. *The Cross and the World*

What we have been saying about the hope that the cross offers to those who have heard but rejected the gospel, offers some clues about the hope that is offered to those who have not rejected it, because they have never heard it, and that category must include, across the continents and down the centuries, the vast majority of people. Paul's questions in Romans certainly apply to them, for: '"Everyone who calls on the name of the Lord will be saved." How, then, can they call on the one they have not believed in? And how can they believe in the one of whom they have not heard? And how can they hear without someone preaching to them?' (Rom. 10:13–14).

[handwritten margin note: one of my props w/ this]

Such people have been kept from responding to the gospel, either by the accidents of history and geography that made the proclamation of the gospel unavailable to them, or because they were shaped and formed by cultural and religious traditions that the gospel never successfully penetrated. For that very reason their situation is less and not more precarious than those of us who have grown up under the sound of the gospel and who have yet responded to it so partially and inconsistently and cannot plead ignorance in our defence. From those to whom so much has been given much shall be required. From a Christian perspective the so-called 'lost millions' of the unevangelised world are to be regarded rather as disadvantaged victims, because, by no fault of their own, they have been deprived of the opportunity of hearing and of responding to the gospel of Christ. The loving offer of that gospel and therefore of that opportunity of response is one of the great motives of the worldwide Christian mission.

(a) Are the Unevangelised Lost?

We must however ask whether one of the assumptions of much of the missionary work of the nineteenth century, especially in more evangelical circles, can be sustained. Part of the urgency of their task for many such missionaries had its source in the conviction that the opportunity of a saving encounter with Christ was confined to this present life, that death fixed everything for ever and all that remained was the final judgement. This consisted entirely of the pronouncing of verdicts and the handing out of

sentences: believers for heaven, unbelievers for hell. In such a
scenario the 'unsaved millions' were lost indeed. Behind such an
attitude there may well be lurking, on the one hand, an over-
reaction to Roman Catholic teaching about purgatory, and on the
other some remnants of the double predestination doctrine in its
fiercest form. Leaving aside the question whether such an attitude to most of his human creation is consonant with the revealed
character of the God and Father of our Lord Jesus Christ who
came to seek and to save what was lost, we may ask whether the
assumption that our relationship to God is irretrievably fixed at
our death is as self-evidently biblical as is often supposed. The
text most often quoted is from Hebrews, which tells us that: 'Just
as man is destined to die once, and after that to face judgement,
so Christ was sacrificed once to take away the sins of many
people; and so he will appear a second time, not to bear sin, but to
bring salvation to those who are waiting for him' (Heb. 9:27–8).
We should notice that here the second coming of Christ is
described in the most positive terms, as the bringing of salvation,
rather than the pronouncing of verdicts. It is indeed true that
that salvation is brought 'to those who are waiting for him', and
nothing is said about anybody else. Nevertheless it is illegitimate
to read into a statement that, when believers die, they encounter
their Saviour, another quite different statement that when unbelievers die they encounter their condemning judge.

We may recollect the point that we made earlier about the
biblical notion of the judge not primarily as the one who pronounces sentences and imposes penalties but as the one who puts
to right in the coming age the things and the people that have
been wrong in the present age. And in particular we recall again
the definitive statement about judgement in John 12, that the
lifting up of Jesus on the cross is in fact the projection into human
history of that final judgement and the outcome of it is that he
will draw everyone to himself.

Within the present age that does not happen. Where the gospel
is preached only some respond, and they very imperfectly, but
where the gospel is not preached, there can be no response at all
to God's once and for all atoning action. But if the crucified and
risen Jesus is indeed at the right hand of the Father and if all
authority in earth and heaven have indeed been committed to
him, then those who have not encountered him in this age will
most certainly encounter him in the next. And certainly they

will encounter him as he has always been, the one who offers release from the past, reconciliation with God and incorporation into his new humanity. The opportunity that has been denied now will be realised then. It will be realised in a way that does not bludgeon people into a forced submission but leaves room for the work of the Spirit to bring them to that free acceptance which, as we have seen, is involved in our incorporation into him.

(i) An Eschatological Encounter

That incorporation can take place only where Christ is known and encountered in his once and for all death and resurrection, but the Spirit of Christ is already at work in people long before he is known, making what happens in this present age a preparation for the encounter that will take place in the age to come. Human culture and human religion, according to Paul in Romans 1, are an ambiguous compound of the work of God and the distortions of a humanity alienated from God by sin: 'They turned the truth of God into a lie and worshipped and served created things rather than the Creator' (Rom. 1:25).

What is truth and what is lie in our culture and religion is revealed to us only in our encounter with Christ who is the Truth. But the Spirit of Christ, even before that encounter, is universally at work fostering and developing what is of God in people until human self-deception and alienation are finally exposed and dealt with in Christ. Lives lived outside the gospel are not wasted or lost if in the end they are exposed to the purifying power of the gospel, because all that is of God in them will be liberated and fulfilled by our eventual incorporation into the new humanity where falsehood is abolished and truth reigns.

(ii) An Awesome Encounter

It is important to see that such a basically positive and affirmative approach to final judgement does not rob it of its radical and penetrating character. It is indeed a fearful thing to fall into the hand of the living God – and all the more fearful when he insists on undertaking the fundamental reconstruction and remaking of the whole human being. The judge who is making all things right will have no truck with wrong. If there is to be a living to God in Christ there must be a dying to sin in Christ, and that sin is so

Purgatory?

intertwined with the depths of us that its expulsion cannot but be shakingly sore. Well does Malachi ask: 'But who can endure the day of his coming? Who can stand when he appears? For he will be like a refiner's fire or a launderer's soap. He will sit as a refiner and purifier of silver; he will purify the Levites and refine them like gold and silver' (Mal. 3:2–3). Through that refiner's fire we all must pass, and, if we know ourselves, we know how fearful that will be.

That fire is endurable because the one who thus refines us loves us and has proved his love on his cross. He purges us so radically because he loves us so completely, not because we are his enemies but because we are, by our incorporation into Christ, his children: 'God is treating you as sons. For what son is not disciplined by his father? If you are not disciplined (and everyone undergoes discipline), then you are illegitimate children and not true sons. Moreover, we have all had human fathers who disciplined us and we respected them for it. How much more should we submit to the Father of our spirits and live!' (Heb. 12:7–10). That discipline for Christians begins in this age, but what happens in this age can be seen as preliminary to that ultimate purging that awaits all who encounter Christ, Christians or not, in the age to come.

(iii) The Impossible Possibility

Equally this positive understanding of the final judgement does not automatically guarantee a universalist outcome. The impossible possibility of encountering the final eschatological manifestation of God's saving love in Jesus and finally defying it and refusing it still remains, albeit in all its illogicality and incomprehensibility. It has been said that God may have abolished capital punishment by the death of his Son but the possibility of suicide still remains. When we are most aware of the residual power of sin in ourselves and our world, that possibility seems all too real, but when we look away from ourselves to the love that has faced and overcome all evil and goes on giving evidence of its presence and power in ourselves and in the world, then hope prevails.

Much in the latter part of this chapter remains highly speculative, as indeed it must on such a subject. It is to be seen only as an attempt to spell out some of the implications of the heart of the

but how can you have suicide w/o an (arminian) will?

gospel which are not speculative: that Jesus Christ died for all and lives for all; that there is ultimate and unquenchable hope for all in his name. 'Praise be to the God and Father of our Lord Jesus Christ! In his great mercy he has given us new birth into a living hope through the resurrection of Jesus Christ from the dead' (1 Pet. 1:3).

10

One Cross – God's Mission of Love

Throughout this book we have been exploring what P. T. Forsyth called the cruciality of the cross. We have been trying to see what follows if we make our own the biblical confession that the cross of Jesus is not only the culmination of his own ministry and the dark door through which he had to pass to the new life of his resurrection, but the great turning point in the history of the human race and of the world in which God revealed himself definitively and acted decisively in a way that breaks the power of evil, both for those who perpetrate it and those who suffer from it. A turning point that opens the door to new life for us all.

1. Faith Seeking Understanding

This has been, as was promised at the beginning, a confessional rather than an apologetic enterprise. We have been presenting not an argument that leads *to* faith, by justifying the gospel of the cross in terms of something other than itself. It has instead been an argument that proceeds *from faith*. We have followed the method of Augustine and Anselm encapsulated in the Latin tag, *fides quaerens intellectum*, faith seeking a fuller and more coherent understanding of that in which it believes. This is, in our present perspective, a faith that begins from a convinced acceptance of the biblical witness to God's atoning act in Christ and seeks to commend itself by the understanding of the human dilemma and God's answer to it that unfolds from that starting point. From any other starting point, as Paul found out long ago, the message of the cross is folly and scandal, and so it still is. But seen in its own light, it offers a vision of God and of his relationships with his people and his world that, in the power of the Holy Spirit, has captured and converted to itself the minds and hearts of people in every age and in every part of the world.

2. *God's Mission of Love*

The story whose universal significance we have been trying to spell out afresh is the story of God's mission of love to the world. Its whole purpose is to tell us in what way God has once and for all expressed and enacted that love and what sort of love it is. To present this story as anything else than a love story is fatally to misrepresent it. Our fundamental criticism of some traditional theologies of atonement has been that by dwelling overmuch on dealing with sin by restoring the balance of justice, by propitiating divine wrath or by exacting required punishment they have obscured the sovereign love from which everything in the story proceeds, which everything in the story expresses and to which everything in the story enables us to return. The only valid summary of the story is that God so loved the world that he gave his only Son (John 3:16) and the final theological implication of the story is that God is love (1 John 4:8, 16).

In 2 Corinthians 5, at the start of a passage that defines Paul's understanding of the cross more clearly and more comprehensively than any other, it is with God's love in Christ that he begins: 'Christ's love compels us, because we are convinced that one died for all, and therefore all died. And he died for all, that those who live should no longer live for themselves but for him who died for them and was raised again' (2 Cor. 5:14–15). If we wanted a concise summary of what we have been trying to say at greater length, although far less adequately, throughout this book, these verses provide it.

They remind us that the love that we are talking about is the 'love of Christ', his gracious love for us that evokes in response our grateful love for him. If we want to know what the love of God is like, we look at the story of the one man who died for all, that all might live through him. We are to be careful to let the story of Jesus define what we mean by God's love and not foist on to that story the many other notions of love that abound in different human cultures and deep down in our own understanding. As we end, we recapitulate some of the distinctive features of this revealed divine love.

(a) A Dynamic and Outgoing Love

The love that expresses itself in the coming and dying of Jesus is not general and mystical; it does not call us into detachment from people and from the eventfulness of history into an esoteric and ethereal eternity. This love is not detached but dynamic; it does not flee from history but rather becomes incarnate within it and exposes itself to all its agonies and ambiguities. Because it is the love of a God who is in himself the mutual and dynamic self-giving of three specific divine persons, the one to the other, his love does not swallow up our specific personhood but rather redeems and affirms it. That is why his love is manifested in a human person and is communicated always from person to person, first in the mission of Jesus and then in the subsequent mission of his people.

The Christian gospel is not about general principles or grand philosophical or theological schemes, but about the meeting of the incarnate divine person with human persons. With Jesus it begins with the invitation to the disciples by the lakeside 'Follow me', and ends when he stands beside a distraught woman who thought he was the gardener and turns her to him by speaking her name. That is why the salvation of the world is accomplished not, as with Plato and the philosophers, by education, or, with Marx and the politicians, by revolution or the more benign exercise of state power, but by the self-offering in love of one man for all people at one specific place and time in history. It follows that the witness in word and action of one person or community of persons to another can best convey the love of Jesus. It is a love to be shared within a communion of persons where each is bidden to eat of his body and drink of his blood.

(b) A Love that Kills and Makes Alive

Furthermore this is a love that both accepts and exposes, that both kills and makes alive. A theology of atonement whose leading category is love is liable to be accused, usually by the grim theologians of divine righteousness, of sentimentality and a lack of awareness of the negative divine reaction to evil and sin – and sometimes with good reason. I hope however that it has been clear throughout that the God who reveals himself to us and acts on our behalf in the cross of Jesus is totally uncompromising in his opposition to evil, whether in its perpetrators or in his victims. In the judgement of his love he exposes it as the crucifying destructive thing that it is. He suffers from it in order that we should die to it, so that its power over us and our responsiveness to it are brought to an end. Divine love is intolerant of everything and everybody that destroys those it loves and it takes radical action to undo the agents of destruction and to deliver those who are being destroyed.

In the cross of Jesus the love of God penetrates behind the fair surfaces that people and societies, including religious societies, present to themselves and to one another and exposes the destroying things that are at the heart of both. 'One died for all and therefore all died.' In the light of the cross the human *status quo* has no secure future. There is that in all of us and in the cultures that surround and shape us that has to die. Mary saw well that the birth of her son meant personal and social revolution, the putting down of the mighty from their seats, the rich being sent empty away. The apocalyptic destruction that occupies so much of the Book of Revelation is the work of the Lamb who is in the midst of the throne; it is a working out on a cosmic scale of the subversion of the *status quo* that Jesus brought about on the cross.

Martin Luther, that chief theologian of the cross, knew that the preaching of the cross causes tumult, as indeed in his day it caused more tumult than he himself could cope with. Crucified love is no easy option; the gospel of the cross is no comfort to the worshippers of easygoing niceness. If we are totally accepted, it is in order that we may be totally changed. The grace of Jesus Christ is no cheap grace that leaves us as we are, but demands that, like a seed, we should fall into the ground and die. If we are delivered, it is only through the heat and burning of his purifying fire.

But such is the genius of the cross that the love that exposes is identical with the love that accepts. When we are not acceptable in ourselves and cannot deliver ourselves from evil, we are incorporated into one who has made our humanity acceptable to the Father precisely by reflecting back to him his own love from the midst of evil, one who has delivered us from evil by taking his love to the very heart of its dark domain and opening up from there the way back to God and to life.

He is the friend of sinners, not because he has compromised with their sin but because he has made himself the way out of it. He provides for us the goodness that we do not have in ourselves and he stands before his Father as a pledge that the life of holy love that is his will through the operation of the Spirit ultimately be ours also: 'He died for all, that those who live should no longer live for themselves but for him who died for them and was raised again.' That is the promise and pledge of his death to his Father and to us. To quote the incomparable Forsyth for the last time:

> Our faith is already present in his oblation ... The effect of his cross is to draw us into a repentance which is a dying with him and therefore a part of the offering in his death; and then it raises us in newness of life to a fellowship of his resurrection. He is thus not only the pledge to us of God's love but the pledge to God of our sure response to it in a total change of will and life.[1]

(c) A Love that Makes us New

All this is credible only if it gives convincing evidence of itself here and now. This is the point at which we can do justice to Paul Fiddes' very proper concern for the power of the crucified and risen Jesus in the present. The claims that we have made for the single event in the past are believable only if the first signs of our incorporation into the new humanity which is Christ's achievement and gift leads to a new expression of love to God, neighbour and enemy in those who confess his cross and his name. We have heightened the stakes by claiming that what Christ offers from his cross is not just forgiveness but a new creation of a new kind of humanity. Making all allowances for the fact that the completion of that new creation is in the eschatological future, that claim remains totally incredible unless we have at least begun to show that love and, in our attitudes and actions, are giving convincing signs of being transformed by it. 'We are being changed into his likeness from one degree of glory to another.' The tense of the verb is present continuous and the transformation of the Christian community needs to be both, if it is going to commend the gospel of the cross.

(d) A Love that is for All

It is to all people everywhere that this love must be thus commended and shown. Jesus on the cross penetrates in his love deeper than the divisions of religion, race, gender, intellectual ability or moral standing. He deals with us all in our basic shared humanity. He deals with us all in our alienation from God and from one another, in our sin and in our suffering. When he draws us to himself we see in him what we have been seeking elsewhere in a multitude of other ways. We see in him that which affirms our personhood and the value of our uniqueness in our own time and place and history. He affirms us by removing what is destructive in us and preserving and transforming what is of God in us. He has room for us, he has grace for us all, those who know him and those many who do not yet know him. He will in his own time and way draw us all to himself us and let us meet one another in a new way, as he did first with John and Mary at his cross.

(e) A Love that Passes Knowledge

Such is his love. Totally for us all and at the same time totally beyond us all. It offers itself from the cross in the midst of the world's mess around us; it comes to the cross but from the mysterious heart of God; from the cross it penetrates every corner of the created world and the human heart. Like the sun, it shines through all the clouds into every place but always from its own place high above us, first on Calvary and then in heaven. It sheds the light and the warmth by which all may live, but it burns in an agony of incandescence that is far beyond us.

To live in the power of the cross is to share in the creative energy of the divine love. Part of our response to it is to give our minds and hearts to comprehend, as far as we can, the incomparable and unquenchable grace that meets us there. We confess Christ crucified as best we can, but we know, as I know ending this book, that he is much greater than any confession, that when all is said, the reality eludes all our speaking and is greater than all our thinking about it.

In the end the theology has to give way to the praying, the explanation to the adoration. And so, author for readers, and I hope, readers for author, we can, with Paul, but commend one another to his love: 'I pray that you, being rooted and established in love, may have power, together with all the saints, to grasp how wide and long and high and deep is the love of Christ, and to know this love that surpasses knowledge – that you may be filled to the measure of all the fullness of God' (Eph. 3:17–19).

Notes

Chapter One: Confessing the One Cross

[1] John McIntyre, *The Shape of Soteriology*, Edinburgh, T & T Clark, 1992, pp 26–7.

[2] Timothy Gorringe, *Cross and Retribution*, Cambridge, CUP, 1996, p 224.

[3] T. S. Eliot, East Coker, from *Four Quartets*.

[4] Jürgen Moltmann, *The Crucified God*, E. T., London, SCM, 1974, p 246.

[5] The same point is made in a slightly different way by Stephen Sykes in *The Story of Atonement*, London, Darton, Longman & Todd, 1997, pp 20–22.

[6] Paul S. Fiddes, *Past Event and Present Salvation, The Christian Idea of Atonement*, London, Darton, Longman and Todd, 1989, p 14.

Chapter Two: One Cross – Four Gospels

[1] Raymond E. Brown, *The Death of the Messiah*, Great Britain, Geoffrey Chapman, 1994, Vols 1 & 2.

[2] Ibid., Vol. 1, p 30.

[3] Ibid., Vol. 1, p 30.

[4] Ibid., Vol. 1, p 34.

[5] C.f. for example John 7:37–9.

[6] Hans Urs von Balthasar, *Mysterium Paschale*, E. T., Edinburgh, T & T Clark, 1990, p 123.

[7] Joachim Jeremias, *The Eucharistic Words of Jesus*, E. T., Oxford, Basil Blackwell, 1955, p 132.

[8] G. B. Caird, *New Testament Theology*, Oxford, Clarendon Press, 1994, p 231.

[9] N. T. Wright, *Jesus and the Victory of God*, London, SPCK, 1996, pp 562–3.

Chapter Three: One Cross – Theodicy or Atonement?

[1] *Book of Common Prayer*, 1662, Prayer of Confession in service of Holy Communion.

[2] Mary Gray in *Scottish Journal of Theology* (1994), Vol. 47, no.2, p 223.

[3] Isaac Rosenberg, 'On Receiving News of the War'.

[4] P. T. Forsyth, *The Justification of God*, London, Duckworth & Co., 1916, p 175.

[5] Cf. J. Moltmann, *The Crucified God*, E. T., London, SCM, 1974, p 174.

[6] Ibid., p 276.

[7] Ibid., p 278.

[8] J. Moltmann, *The Power of the Powerless*, E. T., London, SCM, 1983, pp 118–9.

[9] See, for example, John Calvin, *Institutes of the Christian Religion*, Book 2, chapter 16, paragraph 11, where the same verse is understood in terms of a penal theory of atonement: 'He bore the weight of divine severity, since he was stricken and afflicted by God's hand, and experienced all the signs of a wrathful and avenging God.'

[10] J. Moltmann, *The Spirit of Life*, E. T., London, SCM, 1992, p 136.

Chapter Four: One Cross – The Decisive Deed

[1] Paul S. Fiddes, *Past Event and Present Salvation, The Christian Idea of Atonement*, London, Darton, Longman & Todd, 1989, p 185.

[2] Cf. Hebrews 2:17–18, 4:15.

[3] Paul S. Fiddes, op.cit., p 139.

[4] Ibid., p 106.

[5] Ibid., p 110.

[6] Cf. Matthew 26:28.

[7] Cf. Mark 10:45.

[8] John McIntyre, *The Shape of Soteriology*, Edinburgh, T & T Clark, 1992, pp 26–7.

[9] Colin E. Gunton, *The Actuality of Atonement*, Edinburgh, T & T Clark, 1988, pp 55ff.

[10] In what immediately follows I am indebted to Colin Gunton's discussion of this whole matter, ibid., Chapter 3, pp 53–81.

[11] The Doctrine Commission of the Church of England, *The Mystery of Salvation*, London, Church House Publishing, 1995, pp 139–40.

[12] T. F. Torrance, *The Mediation of Christ* (Second Edition), Edinburgh, T & T Clark, 1992, p 80.

Chapter Five: One Cross – Propitiation or Punishment?

[1] Church of England Doctrine Commission, op.cit., p 126.

[2] Paul Fiddes, op.cit., p 93.

[3] Romans 3:25, Hebrews 2:17, 1 John 2:2, 1 John 4:10.

[4] P. T. Forsyth, *The Work of Christ* (Fifth Impression), London, Independent Press, 1952, pp 88–9.

[5] C. B. Cranfield, *International Critical Commentary: The Epistle to the Romans* (Vol. 1), Edinburgh, T & T Clark, 1975, p 217.

[6] John R. W. Stott, *The Cross of Christ*, London, Inter-Varsity Press, 1986, p 175.

[7] Ibid., p 174.

[8] P. T. Forsyth, op. cit., p 171.

[9] G. B. Caird, *New Testament Theology*, Oxford, Clarendon Press, 1994, p. 137 (footnote).

[10] John R. W. Stott, op. cit., pp 169–70.

11 John Calvin, *Institutes of the Christian Religion*, II, 16,5.

12 Stephen H. Travis, 'Christ as Bearer of Divine Judgement in Paul's Thought about the Atonement' in *Atonement Today* (ed. John Goldingay), London, SPCK, 1995, pp 31–8.

13 Galatians 3:13; 2 Corinthians 5:21; Romans 3:24–6, 5:9–10.

14 Stephen H. Travis, op.cit., p 37.

15 John McIntyre, op.cit., p 44.

16 Karl Barth, *Church Dogmatics*, IV.1, E.T., Edinburgh, T & T Clark, 1956, p 253.

17 Ibid., pp 253–4.

18 C. E. Gunton, *The Actuality of Atonement*, Edinburgh, T & T Clark, 1988, p 188.

19 P. T. Forsyth, op.cit., p 146.

20 W. Pannenberg, *Jesus, God and Man*, E.T., London, SCM, 1968, p 264.

21 P. T. Forsyth, op.cit., pp 146–7.

Chapter Six: One Cross – The Birth of the New Humanity

1 Jeremiah 31:33.

2 John McLeod Campbell, *The Nature of the Atonement* (Second Edition), Macmillan, London, 1886, pp 147–8.

3 Cf. Romans 8:14–17; Galatians 4:6–7.

4 Karl Barth, *Church Dogmatics*, IV.1, E.T., Edinburgh, T & T Clark, 1956, pp 258–9.

5 Cf. Ernst Käsemann, *Commentary on Romans*, E.T., London, SCM, 1980, p 141.

6 C. K. Barrett, *The Second Epistle to the Corinthians* (Black's New Testament Commentaries) London, A & C Black, 1973, p 180.

7 Paul S. Fiddes, op.cit., pp 173–4.

8 Geoffrey Paul, *A Pattern of Faith*, London, Churchman Publishing, 1986, p 61.

9 P. T. Forsyth, op.cit., pp 205–6.

10 John McLeod Campbell, op. cit., p 201.

11 R. C. Moberly, *Atonement and Personality*, London, John Murray, 1907, p 129.

12 P. T. Forsyth, op.cit., p 126.

13 Ibid., p 130.

14 Ibid., p 164.

15 Karl Barth, op.cit., p 280.

16 P. T. Forsyth, op.cit., p 206.

17 For what follows I am indebted to my friend, Professor J. B. Torrance.

Chapter Seven: One Cross – God on the Gallows

1 G. B. Caird, op.cit., p 280.

2 John Heywood Thomas, 'Trinity Logic and Ontology' in *Trinitarian Theology Today*, ed. Christoph Schwöbel, Edinburgh, T & T Clark, 1995, p 78.

[3] For a fuller exposition of this understanding of the work and person of the Spirit, see Tom Smail, *The Giving Gift*, London, Darton, Longman and Todd, 1994, pp 157ff.

[4] John V. Taylor, *The Go-Between God*, London, SCM, 1972, p 102.

[5] T. F. Torrance, *The Mediation of Christ* (New Edition), Edinburgh, T & T Clark, 1992, p 112.

[6] Karl Barth, *Church Dogmatics*, II.1, E.T., Edinburgh, T & T Clark, 1957, pp 257ff.

[7] J. Moltmann, *The Crucified God*, E.T., London, SCM, 1974, p 242.

[8] Hans Urs von Balthasar, *Mysterium Paschale*, E.T., Edinburgh, T & T Clark, 1990, p 108.

[9] J. Moltmann, op.cit., p 243.

[10] Ibid., p 243.

[11] Paul Fiddes, op.cit., p 194.

[12] Hans Urs von Balthasar, op. cit., p 148.

[13] Alan Lewis, 'The Burial of God: Rupture and Resumption as the Story of Salvation' in *Scottish Journal of Theology*, Vol. 40, p 347.

[14] Ibid., p 357.

Chapter Eight: One Cross – Baptism into Communion

[1] R. C. Moberly, op.cit., p 144.

[2] John Baillie, *Our Knowledge of God*, London, Oxford University Press, 1939, pp 181ff.

[3] John McIntyre, op. cit., pp 98ff.

[4] Ibid., p 99.

[5] Ibid., p 99.

[6] R. C. Moberly, op.cit., p 352.

[7] T. F. Torrance, *The Mediation of Christ* (New Edition), Edinburgh, T & T Clark, 1992, p 80.

[8] D. M. Baillie, *The Theology of the Sacraments*, London, Faber & Faber, 1957, p 115.

[9] Ezekiel 37:1–14.

[10] R. C. Moberly, op.cit., p 152.

[11] W. Pannenberg, *Systematic Theology*, Vol. 2, Edinburgh, T & T Clark, 1994, pp 431ff.

Chapter Nine: One Cross – For the Whole World

[1] J. Jeremias, *The Eucharistic Words of Jesus*, E.T., Oxford, Basil Blackwell, 1955, p 123.

[2] Quoted in C. E. B. Cranfield, *The Gospel According to St Mark*, Cambridge, CUP, 1959, p 227.

[3] John McLeod Campbell, op. cit., p 54.

[4] Ibid., p.56.

[5] *Book of Common Prayer*, 1662.

[6] Karl Barth, *Church Dogmatics*, IV, 3.1, E.T., Edinburgh, T & T Clark, 1961, p 478.

Chapter Ten: One Cross – God's Mission of Love

[1] P. T. Forsyth, *The Work of Christ* (Fifth Edition), London, Independent Press, 1952, pp 193–4.

INDEX

death 138ff
Dodd, C. H. 83, 89

Eucharist 146–8
expiation 89–90

faith 156, 183
Fiddes, Paul 17, 18, 62ff, 83, 106–7, 136, 149
forgiveness 78, 107
Forsyth, P. T. 45, 86, 87, 98, 111, 118–19, 186

God the Father
  his attributes 87–8
  his initiating love 85ff
  his mourning 133
  his restorative justice 95
  his wrath 81ff
  relationship to the crucified Jesus 46–7
  resurrection as the F's judgement 118, 143
Gorringe, Timothy 4
Gray, Mary 41
Gunton, Colin 95

Hebrews, Letter to the 72–6, 90, 110–11, 122–3, 136, 145
Holocaust 46ff
humanity
  Christ's identification with 103ff
  its transformation 109–10
  new humanity 37–8, 88, 100ff, 151, 153, 160

incorporation into Christ 143ff
  by faith 156–7
  in the Eucharist 146–8
  in baptism 144–5
  into a community 158–9
  into Christ's death and resurrection 157–8

our free act 161–2
personal 154–5
sacraments of incorporation 143–4
work of Holy Spirit 159–61

Jeremias, J. 34, 164
Jesus Christ
  as Messiah of Israel 145–6
  as victim 50–2
  at the Last Supper 34ff
  cry of desolation 22–3
  his atoning obedience 111
  his baptism 30–2
  his confession 116–17
  his death for all 164ff
  his dependence on Abba 100
  his divinity 120ff
  his intercession 113–14, 116
  his priesthood 72–5, 110, 154
  his understanding of his death 30ff
  his unity with the Father 124ff
  his vicarious work 64, 101, 148ff
  in Gethsemane 33–4
  king in the kingdom 32–3
  our contemporary 145–6
  relation of his life, death, resurrection 14, 29–30
  seven words from the cross 20–1
judgement
  borne in our place 151
  in John 25
  its reality 81ff
  meaning of 101, 109, 116–19, 179–81
justification 64ff

Last Supper
  and the rebirth of humanity 119
  as inauguration of the New Covenant 36–7
  as Passover 35, 79